THE DROPOUT PREVENTION SPECIALIST WORKBOOK

OXFORD WORKSHOP SERIES

SCHOOL SOCIAL WORK ASSOCIATION OF AMERICA

Series Advisory Board

THE DROPOUT PREVENTION SPECIALIST WORKBOOK

A How-To Guide for Building the Skills and Competencies for Addressing the School Dropout Crisis

Howard M. Blonsky

OXFORD WORKSHOP SERIES

OXFORD
UNIVERSITY PRESS

OXFORD
UNIVERSITY PRESS

Oxford University Press is a department of the University of Oxford. It furthers
the University's objective of excellence in research, scholarship, and education
by publishing worldwide. Oxford is a registered trade mark of Oxford University
Press in the UK and certain other countries.

Published in the United States of America by Oxford University Press
198 Madison Avenue, New York, NY 10016, United States of America.

Library of Congress Control Number: 2019031790
ISBN 978–0–19–009084–5

1 3 5 7 9 8 6 4 2

Printed by Marquis, Canada

Contents

I

Introduction

> The dropout problem is one we cannot afford to ig-
> nore. The stakes are too high—for our children, for our
> economy, for our Country. It's time for all of us to come
> together—parents and students, principals and teachers,
> business leaders and elected officials—to end America's
> dropout crisis.
>
> —President Barack Obama

The reality of students dropping out of school prior to graduation, some as young as elementary age, is still of crisis proportions in the United States. The many reasons for this crisis in American education are very complex, and both the causes and the solutions are numerous and often quite interrelated. Too few individuals working in schools have been designated as *dropout prevention specialists* (DPS), and there is a need to train the next generation of individuals who will assume this very important role. Many books and articles have been written about the causes of dropout and some have recommended solutions, but there has been little information published regarding how to actually go about doing this complex job. This is the reason for developing this workbook. Emphasis will be placed on helping the DPS to become a school-wide catalyst in institutionalizing key prevention and intervention strategies that meet the needs of a diverse population. Let's start by taking a look at some of the reasons why students drop out.

The Dropout Prevention Specialist Workbook. Howard M. Blonsky, Oxford University Press (2020).
© Oxford University Press.
DOI: 10.1093/oso/9780190090845.003.0008

Possible Predictors/Factors in Students Dropping Out

Personal Factors of the Student

- Low self-esteem and expectations of self
- Boredom
- Social isolation (few friends)
- Negative peer influence (i.e., gangs, drugs, alcohol)
- History of running away from home
- Resentful of authority
- Behavior problems at home and/or in the community
- Lack of involvement in school and community activities
- Substance or alcohol use and abuse
- Perceived need to work to help support their family or themselves
- Emotional problems
- Frequent or chronic health problems
- Eating disorders: anorexia, bulimia, obesity
- Lack of goals or unrealistic goals
- Lack of belief in the benefit of "the system" for their future
- Difficulty relating to adults
- Pregnancy and/or parenting (lacks childcare)
- Language issues

Student Factors Related to School

- Academic failure (fails one or more courses per semester)
- Behind in credits, and the district does not have credit recovery options
- Excessive absences/truancies
- Twenty or more absences in kindergarten or first grade
- A student who failed one or more grades in any school they may have attended
- Two or more years behind in reading and/or mathematics
- One or more grade retentions
- Over age for grade level they are in
- Lack of involvement in school activities
- Feeling of not belonging and social isolation
- Behavior problems at school, including conflict with teachers
- Low test scores (state, district, classroom-level)
- Failed minimum standards
- Unmet special education needs/learning difficulties
- Lack of continuity in educational programs and/or schools

The Dropout Prevention Specialist Workbook

- Perceived lack of caring and personalization from the school
- Perceived negative messages from the school
- Lack of support for language/acculturation process/needs
- Immigrant students who started school later in their native country and did not catch up with their age/peer group in the United States

Family Factors
- Lack of family support for the importance of school
- Members of the family are school dropouts
- Parental separation, divorce, or split home
- Stressful home life/family crisis
- Frequent family moves
- Inadequate housing
- Homeless
- Family substance abuse
- Not enough family income to support the family (including unemployment benefits)
- Low educational attainment levels of caregivers as role models
- Lack of communication with the school due to language barriers
- Recent death in the home or terminally ill parent
- Care of a younger siblings (family need for childcare)
- Child abuse and neglect
- Poor communication between family and the school

School Structure/System Factors
- Negative climate and culture of the school
- Large, impersonal school that lacks supports and accommodations for students
- Lack of an orderly start of the school year
- Lack of a comprehensive orientation program for new students
- Lack of collaborative teamwork among the staff
- Isolation of teachers
- Lack of positive, cooperative relationships between and among students, staff, parents, and administrators
- School rules that that are inconsistent or not fairly or equitably enforced
- Negative messages to students
- Lack of programs to ease transitions
- Lack of follow-up on truant youth or those who have already dropped out

Community-Related Factors
- Lack of responsive community support services
- Fragmentation of resources and services
- Lack of preventative efforts: overemphasis on crisis response or after problems occur
- Lack of linkages between community programs/resources and schools

Vision/Leadership Barriers
- Lack of a strong belief among district leaders that poor attendance and the dropout numbers can be improved
- Lack of leadership in implementing the most creative practices and policies

According to Robert Balfanz, the majority of factors contributing to students dropping out can be categorized into four groups[1]:

- *Life events*: Students drop out because of an event or need outside of school. Examples include pregnancy, out of home placement, aging out of foster care, caring for a family member, or needing to work to support themselves or their families.
- *Fade outs*: Students drop out because they no longer see the point of staying in school. Often these are students with decent grades and attendance records who, at some point, become bored, frustrated, or disillusioned with school and believe they can make it in life on their own without a high school diploma.
- *Push outs*: Students may be viewed as behavioral problems or low achievers, and/or they seldom attend school. Once these students reach the legal dropout age, their schools may apply administrative rules—related to suspensions, inadequate credits earned by a certain age, or chronic absenteeism—to remove them from school or transfer them to another school.
- *Failure to succeed in school*: Students drop out of school because they do not pass enough courses or earn enough credits to be promoted to the next grade. Many of these dropouts begin to fall off the path to graduation in the middle grades, when they begin to fail courses, miss a lot of school, or misbehave. The key point for promotion—or failure—is from the 9th to 10th grades. These students often have to

repeat the entire 9th grade and, without any supports, do no better the second time around. After repeated attempts to succeed in school, these students begin to believe that they will never succeed in school, so they drop out.

"Dropping out itself might be better viewed as a process of disengagement from school, perhaps for either academic or social reasons that culminates in the final act of leaving."[2] Some authors refer to this gradual disengagement as a "dimming" process, as in a light that slowly burns out.

> Every fall, some 3.5 million young people enter the 8th grade. Over the succeeding four years, more than 505,000 of them drop out—an average of more than 2,805 per day of the school year. Every single day, more than 70 school buses drive out of America's schoolyard, filled with students who will not return. We all pay the price.[3]

Dropout Prevention Specialist Roles and Responsibilities

The roles and responsibilities listed in this section are important if you are to make a significant dent in the dropout problem in your school, your school district, and/or your community. Each item starts with a code to indicate the level of service, either client level or system level (CL, client/student level; S1, school site level; S2, both site and district levels; S3, larger community, city, state, federal level).

Job Description for a DPS

1. S1: Raise the awareness of school personnel, caregivers, community partners, and local businesses of the effects of chronic absenteeism, truancy, and other challenges associated with poor attendance and dropping out of school.
2. CL, S1: Identify and respond to grade-level and pupil subgroup patterns of chronic absence or truancy.
3. S1: Serve as a member on school-based teams, such as the School Coordinated Care Team (SGGT) (aka, student assistance team [SAT], coordination of services team [COST], multidisciplinary team [MDT], student success team [SST], or the school attendance review team [SART]) as they address the attendance, achievement, and behavioral concerns of students.

---

4. S1, S2, S3: Identify and address factors contributing to chronic absenteeism and habitual truancy, including disciplinary actions such as suspension and expulsion.

5. CL, S1: Ensure that students with attendance problems are identified as early as possible to provide applicable support services and interventions.

6. CL, S1, S2, S3: Evaluate the effectiveness of strategies implemented to reduce chronic absenteeism, truancy rates, and the number of dropouts.

7. CL,S1: Work and collaborate with teachers and other school-based personnel to identify students who are potential dropouts.

8. S1, S2: Assist in designing and implementing a comprehensive plan for your school or district to reduce the dropout rate.

9. C1, S1, S2: Assist in the creation and implementation of re-entry and other credit recovery options.

10. C1, S1: Design and implement individualized intervention plans with strategies and defined responsibilities to address the needs of identified students and, when appropriate, their caregivers.

11. C1, S1: Promote co-curricular and extracurricular activities that increase pupil connectedness and bonding to the school, such as leadership opportunities, cross-age tutoring, mentoring, the arts, service learning, and/or athletics.

12. S1: Recruit, train, and monitor mentors as part of a comprehensive dropout prevention program.

13. S1, S2: Utilize the resources of classroom teachers, the larger school environment, the home, and the community to be part of a comprehensive plan to address students' needs. This is often referred to as "the broad range of interventions" (a more complete description can be found in Chapter 3).

14. S1, S2: Monitor the school performance of identified "at risk" students in the area of academics, attendance, and behavior.

15. CL: Contact and communicate directly with caregivers on a regular basis to ensure their awareness of and involvement in their child's school performance and attendance. Help gain the support of their child's participation in various opportunities, services, and supports that may be of value to them and have the potential to deter them from dropping out.

16. CL: Conduct home visits to join with caregivers, and facilitate communication between the school and the home.
17. S1, S2: Maintain accurate data, records, and case files to document the activities conducted and the services provided to students and their families.
18. S1, S2: Collect, interpret, and use student attendance data to develop strategies addressing dropout prevention.
19. S1, S2: Utilize the potential and power of peers in school activities as mediators, as cross-age tutors, in buddy programs, and in other activities.
20. S1, S2: Research model programs and funding opportunities for dropout prevention.
21. S1, S2, S3: Summarize, interpret, and disseminate current developments in dropout prevention through reading professional journals, participating in professional development, and becoming involved in professional organizations.
22. C1: Recognize and, when appropriate, reward students who achieve excellent or improved attendance.

This range of services/interventions represents efforts that might be undertaken by the DPS either working as an individual or, preferably, as a member of a team. The hope is that the DPS becomes a catalyst/change agent in the school and/or district to assist in the development and implementation of a comprehensive dropout prevention and recovery program in their school and/or district. All of this starts with a focus on one student who is showing at-risk patterns that may lead him or her to drop out of school. *Efforts with each and every student are truly at the heart of this very important role. Whether working at the client/student level and/or working at the system level, these are most important endeavors.*

Not a One-Person Job

Many years ago I was part of the dropout prevention program in California, a program that funded more than 330 schools to address dropout prevention efforts at the school and district levels. The legislation that generated the funding for this effort—the only such legislation ever enacted in California— was meant, in part, to fund a person called an Outreach Consultant in each school who would assume many of the responsibilities just listed for a DPS. This cadre of good and well-meaning people did important work on behalf

---

of their students and achieved some significant success, as determined by outside evaluators. In the conferences that were convened to bring together a team from each of the funded schools, many of the Outreach Consultants (or DPS) complained that school staff would often say to them, "the efforts to curb dropouts in our schools is your job, not ours . . . we have lots of other things to do." How wrong they were. Curbing the stem of students at risk of becoming dropouts is everybody's job, not just one person's, no matter how well-meaning and hard-working that person may be. I have always said that the best form of work in schools is *teamwork*.

The effort to curb the number of students at risk for dropping out has to be a school-wide effort, and yes, a district-level and district-wide effort, and yes, a city-wide effort, and yes, a state-wide effort, and yes, an effort made by the entire country. The fact that only about 60–75% of students in the United States graduate high school—and in some cities and areas, this number is around 50%—is a national disgrace. It will take all of our concerted efforts to improve these dismal numbers. The future for those who drop out prior to receiving a high school diploma or GED, often considered one of the most important benchmarks in our society, is quite limited, and although there are some exceptions, the costs to society over the long run are staggering.

Relationships, Relationships, Relationships

The first and most important job of the DPS is to develop as many relationships as possible if their work as a school-wide catalyst has a chance to be successful. This often involves finding the "key" to a connection with each and every person. Social workers talk about the professional "use of self," meaning that if there is something about you, your interests, your passions, your hobbies, your background, or anything else that may help you to develop a relationship with the person whom you are seeking a connection, then you must use that.

Many years ago I was working in a middle school and there was a man who was in the role of a dean of students. He had a reputation of being a sort of "tough guy," someone who was hard on the students. One day I went into his office to talk with him about a particular student, and I noticed he was working on something that looked like knitting. I asked him what he was doing, and he said that he was doing macrame, something I knew nothing about. He told me it was a hobby of his and it helped him get through the day by keeping his hands occupied. I asked him if he would consider making something for me with macrame. He said he would. I told him I would pay him for a necklace made of macrame, and we agreed that he would do this for me. About a week later he called me into his office, and low and behold, there was my necklace. It looked very nice, and I told him how excited I was to have it. I paid him the amount we had agreed to, took my necklace, and left. After that day, we had a great working relationship. In all honesty, I really did not need a macrame necklace, but by recognizing his skill in this area and agreeing with him to make a necklace for me, I had found the "key" to developing a relationship with him. From that point forward, he was a friend and a colleague I could easily talk to and work collaboratively with for the benefit of the students we mutually were responsible to serve. This true story is an example of trying to find a key to developing a working relationship with as many team workers as possible.

Disaggregate the Data

We can learn an enormous amount about what is going on in our school or in our district through a careful analysis of the data that are available regarding test scores and subtest scores, attendance and truancy rates, suspension numbers, credits earned, and the number of F's and D's given to the students. Through the process of breaking down these data, often referred to as "disaggregating" the data, patterns can be found that can help us to address what is going on with a particular group of students. While we frequently will be working with one student at a time showing "at-risk" patterns, finding trends in a group or groups of students can set the school or district on a course to approach this as a much larger systemic problem. Most school districts take period-by-period attendance, and the marked scan sheets completed by teachers when they take roll are fed into a mainframe computer that has the ability to do many things with this valuable information. The mainframe computer can print out each individual student's attendance history, class period by class period. It can also print out the names of students who are attending a certain percentage of the time (i.e., 90–100%, 80–90%, 70–80%, 60–70%, 60%, or below). These lists should be given to the counselor of record for the student and to the school attendance review team (SART). These names represent those students who are most in need of intervention before the pattern becomes even worse, often leading to yet another dropout statistic if the underlying issues that are causing the problem are not addressed.

An example of disaggregated data that might show a *systemic problem*—a problem that is shared by many students and that is effecting their attendance—is as follows. An analysis of disaggregated data shows that 50% of African American students are failing Algebra 1 in the 9th grade, causing these students to start to fall behind in their credits and making them "at risk" for eventually dropping out. Armed with these data, it is possible to develop a program to address this "systemic" pattern. For example, a tutorial program in algebra, perhaps one that provides upper-grade students to tutor younger students, could be developed for those students who have failed the course. Allowing the students who failed Algebra 1 to repeat the course before being programmed into Algebra 2 in the second semester of the 9th grade (a possibility that did not exist in the district where I worked) until the following school year after the student has also failed Algebra 2. There are many examples such as this, and the DPS can find more of them by "disaggregating the data" that can be literally at their fingertips and by working with the district's tech department. This process is also referred to as a "cycle of inquiry" that leads to a "data-driven improvement process." Of course, it is not expected that the DPS is the only staff member who pursues this cycle of inquiry, but the DPS can ask the right questions of the principal, the district research and evaluation department, the testing coordinator at the school, and others who are involved in data collection and analysis.

Questions to think about:

1. Does your school regularly examine student data, particularly in regard to student attendance, behavior, and achievement?
2. Does your school set annual goals in the areas of attendance, student attitude, and achievement based on an examination of the data?
3. Does the data analysis in your school include student performance by subgroups?
4. Is there an ongoing improvement plan that your school uses that includes assessment and the setting of quantifiable goals?
5. Are data used throughout the year to identify areas of weakness among the students, as well as identifying concepts that should be re-taught for student mastery?
6. Are the data for raising the academic achievement scores of 9th-grade students made available to teachers who are teaching 9th-grade students?

Where Is the Money?

Many times the school or the district has funding coming from special grants or for defined programs or services from the city, state, or federal government or from charitable foundations. At the school site level these funds are sometimes overseen by the *school site council* (SSC). It is a good idea for the DPS to put him- or herself forward as a candidate for one of the positions on the SSC and/or to attend meetings of this group to learn about such funds. Hopefully, if given the opportunity, the DPS can speak to the student needs that can be addressed by some of these funds. Another avenue for influence is the *leadership team* at the school. This would be another good place for DPS to put themselves forward as spokespersons for addressing the needs of students who are falling behind and are at risk for dropping out.

Districts can be hesitant to share information about funds that do not have the focus of defined responsibilities or populations. In California the funding for a former program to curb the number of dropouts in some 330 schools was "block granted" in 2006, which essentially took away all of the regulations and expectations of the program. The legislature, in their "wisdom," determined that the local school district (local control) was the best source to know how this money should be spent. The money that was generated from this so called categorical program still flows to the districts that originally received this funding, but, to the best of my knowledge, very little, if any of these funds, currently go toward dropout prevention efforts. The funds go right from the state into the general fund of the district, and it seems as though this money is used for all kinds of special projects or salaries that have nothing to do with dropout prevention. What a shame. Keep in mind that school districts generate most of their state funding from average daily attendance (ADA) numbers. In California, in order to qualify for the approximate $40–50 a day per student, the school must see the nose of this student in school at least once a day. If a youngster comes to school for one or maybe two periods a day and then "cuts" the rest of the day, the district can still claim that the student was in school, making the district eligible to receive the ADA. Thus, every student whose attendance we can help to improve or who we can prevent from dropping out can yield more money for the district, and more money from this increase in revenue can go to hire more people to do this important work. In many ways, we can earn our own salaries through the number of students we keep in school who otherwise might have dropped out.

Some states give money to a school district for the entire coming school year based on the number of students who are enrolled in the "10-day count" (the first 10 days of the school year). Many people feel that this way of pulling down state money is a "disincentive" to keep students in school because, once they have their operating funds for the year, the school or district no longer has to work hard to keep students in school or to try to re-enter them once they have been absent for long periods of time or have dropped out. Unfortunately, some schools and districts tend to "write off" students they see as troublesome or who might bring down their test scores, and these institutions don't put out the effort to keep them in school once they show poor attendance patterns. It seems that districts who "earn" their state funds from the number of students attending day by day throughout the year have a better incentive to keep students in school.

Perseverance Can and Does Pay Off

Maria was a 12th-grade student in advanced placement classes, slated to graduate in just a few short months, when, all of a sudden, she just disappeared from the school without a word. Our district had a policy that if a student had not been seen in 15 days, he or she would be dropped from the rolls. I regularly checked the names of truant students, and I noticed her name on the list. When I checked her stellar record, it seemed strange that she would have just disappeared without even a word. I started making calls to her home, over and over again, until one evening I was able to catch up with Maria. I asked her to come to the school and meet with me. When we did meet, I asked her what had been going on and why she was not coming to school. The story went something like this. An aunt and uncle owned a mom-and-pop store grocery store. One night a man with a gun came in to rob the store. Her family did not want to turn over any of their hard-earned money, so they resisted. The robber shot the aunt, a mother of two children, leaving her dead on the floor. When Maria heard about what had happened, she immediately ran to her relatives' home and assumed responsibility for taking care of the two young children. School just faded into the background as she worked day and night to deal with this family tragedy and to care for the children.

I was very impressed with her commitment and caring for her niece and nephew, and I wanted to find some way to help her if I could. I reached out to her teachers and told them enough to gain their empathy and support. They agreed to give her independent study work to make up what she had missed and gave her a chance to pass their classes. She did just that and came back a few weeks later with all of the completed assignments, which were turned over to her teachers. She passed all of her classes and was able to graduate with the rest of her class.

This is a true story, and I share it with you to make the point that our efforts to uncover why students are missing school are very important. I call this "peeling the onion," leaving no stone unturned until the often many-faceted uncovered with understood. Perseverance can and does pay off, and it can make a tremendous difference to the lives of children and youth who are facing a myriad of social, emotional, familial, and other issues, at times through no fault of their own.

Some districts drop a student from the rolls after 15 days of unexcused absence, and little or no follow-up is done if the student is considered as having "dropped out." Unfortunately, some school staff don't go the "extra mile," taking the time and effort to pursue the reasons that students are falling behind and missing a lot of school. This is unfortunate, but those who assume the role of a DPS must think and act differently, putting the needs of students at the forefront.

Questions to think about:

1. How does the role of the DPS differ from other support staff in the school?
2. Of the factors listed for why students drop out of school, which ones does the school have the most potential to influence in a positive way?
3. What strategies will help you establish credibility with teachers, parents, students, and staff in your role as a DPS?
4. What can the school potentially learn from disaggregating the data?
5. Do you see any groups of students in your school who have similar issues/patterns that may lead to dropping out? How can you go about identifying these groups of students?
6. How can you contribute to the building of opportunities, services, and supports once these needs have been identified?

2

The Importance and Benefits of Teams

It is hoped that your school already has a number of team structures, such as the School Coordinated Care Team, (SCCT), (aka, student assistance team (SAT), coordination of services team (COST), multidisciplinary team (MDT), Student Success Team (SST) and the School Attendance Review Team (SART) in place. Teams such as these are very important for a variety of reasons:

1. They join together the important student support personnel at the school.
2. There is an opportunity to hear each other's perspectives and thinking in the development of action plans (also referred to as *service plans* or *intervention plans*).
3. They allow for the sharing of responsibilities. This serves to ensure that one or two people don't carry the load of implementing all of the efforts on behalf of students.
4. They ensure coordination of effort so that duplication of services is avoided. It is clear to everyone what services and resources are being provided to each student, whose responsibility it is to provide a particular intervention, and by what time it will occur.
5. They ensure that follow-up dates are defined to monitor whether the planned strategies, actions, and interventions have taken place and what their effect was.
6. They prevent people from working in isolation.

The Benefits of Effective Teaming

When approaching a new task, such as serving on an educational team, most people experience anxieties and apprehensions about how effectively they will perform in this new and challenging role. Working as a team member

The Dropout Prevention Specialist Workbook. Howard M. Blonsky, Oxford University Press (2020).
© Oxford University Press.
DOI: 10.1093/oso/9780190090845.003.0008

often involves a change in traditional ways of working and the loss of what may be perceived as the advantages of working alone. It involves sharing with others, and it may be both physically and emotionally draining. It may require giving up a certain amount of "territorial imperatives," and it also involves exposure. Although these anxiety-producing elements are to be understood and respected, all of them have been experienced and overcome by many others who have approached the new and exciting venture of serving on a student support team. Table 2.1 lists some "teamed" and "un-teamed" characteristics, and Box 2.1 lists some of the pros and cons of committee work.

Nothing speaks better than success itself to counteract initial misgivings. As the team proceeds with its work, the awareness of improved communication, shared responsibility, and mutual support can serve to generate a sense of togetherness and purpose. By proceeding in their work with students, staff, and families, and by observing the positive effects that can be achieved, team members can renew a sense of accomplishment in their work. Team efforts can and do bring the same satisfaction we hope our youngsters will achieve as they overcome their own anxieties and roadblocks on their road to mastery.

In addition to the positive effects experienced by the staff, the effect of coordinated planning and interventions can have profound implications for the child and his or her family. Far too often, a child's progress through the schools and other service institutions of the larger society is a hit-or-miss experience. Many times only those who manifest their concerns most directly—and often negatively—receive services, often when it is very late to make a difference.

Table 2.1 "Teamed" versus "un-teamed" characteristics

Terms applicable to "teamed efforts"	Terms that may be applicable to "un-teamed" efforts
Coordinated	Uncoordinated
Integrated	Disintegration
Interdependent	Vacuum
Shared support	Fragmented
Support network	Isolation
Can lead to:	Can lead to:
Improved functioning	Dysfunction

Things People Like About Committees When They Function Well

- The role of the committee is clearly defined.
- Time is carefully controlled. Meetings start and end on time. Enough time is allowed to complete the committee's work.
- People listen and respect each others' opinions.
- The facilitator and committee members are well prepared. Materials are prepared and available to everyone in advance, if possible.
- Members are qualified and interested. They want to be part of the committee. A definite commitment exists.
- Interruptions are avoided or held to a minimum.
- Good minutes and records are kept so that decisions are not lost.
- Periodically, the committee stops and assesses its own performance. Needed improvements are worked out.
- Committee members feel they are given some kind of recognition for their committee efforts.

Reasons Why People Do Not Like to Serve on Committees

- The leadership/facilitation is poor. The facilitator fails to keep the discussion on the subject and to keep things moving in the appropriate direction.
- The goals are unclear.
- Assignments are not taken seriously by committee members. There is an apparent lack of commitment.
- Discussions of concerns are unproductive, with no conclusions or decisions.
- Often one person or a "clique" dominates. Some members talk and push for their positions, leaving others to wonder why they are even there.
- Committee members are unprepared, including the facilitator of the meeting. The agenda is not prepared, and materials that need to be there are not available. Someone has not done his or her homework.

- No action is taken. The committee spends a lot of time in discussion without coming up with specific items that lead to action.
- People often have hidden agendas—such as personal axes to grind.
- Members get into discussions that only one or two think are important.

Either by design or default, public education is the one institution of society that reaches the great majority of children and their attendant difficulties. By joining our collective efforts, we can provide that preventive and early intervention thrust that is so necessary, especially with students who are showing patterns that could lead to dropping out if the signs are not caught early and addressed.

The dropout prevention specialist (DPS) cannot work in a vacuum. By serving as a member on one or more student support teams or even chairing some team functions, the DPS fulfills a crucial role in addressing the needs of many students.

The Characteristics of an Effective Team

To be effective, a team must:

- Have a clear understanding of its goals
- Have achieved a high degree of communication and understanding among its members
- Be able to initiate and carry out effective decision making, carefully securing the commitment of all members to important decisions.

Questions to think about:

1. If you have ever served on a team, what did you like about it and what didn't you like about it?
2. What can you, as the DPS, do to contribute to the smooth functioning of the team(s) and making them more effective?
3. What role do you see yourself playing on the teams you will serve on?

What is most important is that each person is recognized for his or her contribution and perspective. It is very important that everyone is "heard" throughout the process, including the parent/guardian and the student. In the next chapter, let's take a look at the specifics of how these team structures are organized and some best practices in making these work.

3

Team Structures

The School Coordinated Care Team (SCCT), Student Success Team (SST), School Attendance Review Team (SART), and Student Attendance Review Board (SARB)

Care Team

I particularly like the "care" team's title in that it implies caring for the students—the reason we are all doing this kind of work.

The purposes of the care team are as follows:

1. Provide coordinated intervention/action planning on behalf of students
2. Ensure that people are not working at cross purposes
3. Make sure that the perspectives and expertise of various disciplines and individuals are heard and considered
4. Follow-up on the intervention/action plans of students who had previously been brought before the care team
5. Consider any trends (learned from the disaggregated data) reflected in the referred population as well as in the general school population; this should lead to a discussion about the need for developing additional programs, services, and resources, and how to access or develop and implement them

The school coordinated care team (SCCT) is a venue where all of the school's support personnel come together on a regular basis, preferably every week or at least every other week. Members of this team typically include an administrator, a school social worker, school psychologist, school nurse, special education representative, parent liaison, school counselor(s), dropout

The Dropout Prevention Specialist Workbook. Howard M. Blonsky, Oxford University Press (2020).
© Oxford University Press.
DOI: 10.1093/oso/9780190090845.003.0008

prevention specialist (DPS), and others as available at the school. Someone is selected as the facilitator of the meeting, although this role is fluid and can be shared on a revolving basis among members of the team. It is very important that members of the Care team commit to regular attendance even if they are not working full time at the school. The Care team meeting, unlike a student success team (SST) meeting, does not include the student and his or her caregivers. Each member of the Care team is asked to sign an *Oath of Confidentiality*, and, by doing so, they agree not to share confidential information about the student and his or her family outside the structure of the meeting. Sensitive student and family information will be discussed at Care team meetings, and, at times, the meeting may include representatives of school-based or school-linked community personnel. By having everyone sign an Oath of Confidentiality, they are stating, under penalty of law, that they will not divulge any information related to this student or family outside of the Care team meetings. The signed Oath documents will be kept at the front of the Care team binder along with copies of the care/action plan documents for each individual student.

The facilitator receives referrals of new students of concern to add to the agenda for discussion at the next meeting. The facilitator is responsible for seeing that all expected/required documents are in place so that the discussion moves smoothly and stays on point. In addition to new students of concern, the agenda typically includes students who have come before the committee before and are scheduled for follow-up review. The agenda also includes services and program coordination issues, important dates for meetings, and other important events for members of the committee to put on their calendars.

For each student who is discussed, a care/action plan form will be completed. A copy is kept in the Care team binder, and a copy is provided to each person in attendance. Each plan will contain the names of the person(s) responsible for each of the "interventions/actions," the date by which the action is to occur, and the date to bring this student back for follow-up review. There are many versions of this form such and creating one to fit your school and your reality is strongly suggested. (See sample forms and frequently asked questions to support the Care team process in the Appendix.)

Presentation of a Student for Discussion to the Care Team

For discussion of a student to move forward, those who are responsible for presenting the student to the team should be prepared and ready to do so. It is very important for certain documents be "at the table." These are as follows:

1. Referral form completed by the referring party
2. The students cum folder
3. A completed cum folder review form
4. Teacher input forms from each teacher and each subject
5. Attendance record, scholarship record, and current grades in progress, credits earned
6. History of any disciplinary infractions
7. Work samples, if appropriate

The presenter should be prepared to discuss in the following order:

1. The strengths of the student
2. Significant background information
3. Current issues and concerns
4. What has already been attempted and what the results have been
5. Ideas and/or direction of where to go from this point forward
6. Possible interventions (actions) in the classroom, the larger school environment, the home, and the community

After being presented with the referral and documentation, the members of the team "brainstorm" on what the next step or the action plan should contain. The action plan could take a variety of tracks, such as scheduling a SST meeting, providing suggestions to the student's caregivers, instituting a change of program, initiating a home visit, convening a meeting of all the student's teachers with the student and caregiver present, listing credit recovery options that will be offered to the student, or referring the student to the school attendance review team (SART), mental health services, a mentor program, or the like. The Care team may decide on the package of interventions and decide to monitor them, or they can refer the student to another team structure. It is worth emphasizing again that the Care team will only be successful if the time is allocated carefully. Once I went to a school to sit in on a Care team meeting and the entire time was spent discussing one student. If the discussion does not move along in the manner suggested, other needy students may be deprived of a discussion and service planning on their behalf.

Interventions

The following defines the broad range of interventions that can and should be considered at the care team level, in an SST or SART meeting, or in the case management phase.

The Classroom

Teachers have a difficult job. Children's needs, learning styles, trigger points, and motivators are so diverse that no single teacher can provide all of the answers. The spirit of the team structure is a collaborative one in which members of the team are encouraged to share ideas and strategies with one another. It is useful if the team you are serving on maintains a "library" of resources and strategies that have worked in the past. There are numerous manuals available. One such resource is the Pre-Referral Intervention manual that lists numerous specific ideas for almost any issue presented in the classroom. With regard to classroom interventions, if these are part of the service/care plan, it might be a good idea for a peer teacher, if one is a member of the team, to be the one who assumes this responsibility as he or she will most likely be the best one to work with other teachers on behalf of the student.

The Larger School Environment

To the extent that the school has developed a range of innovative opportunities, services, and supports within the school environment, the team and the DPS have school-wide resources from which to choose as part of the action/Care plan. (This will be discussed more fully in Chapter 5). The positive relations that are developed between staff members and the student and the range of choices made available to the student to develop interests and skills in art, music, athletics, etc. can go a long way in developing or reinforcing self-esteem and keeping the student in school.

The DPS needs to be familiar with such details as who the contact person is; any special eligibility requirements; and the time, place, and duration of the service or program the student is referred to. Students should be encouraged to seek out this information for themselves, but the DPS should be ready to fill in any details that may be missed by the student. The DPS/case manager should check in with the student after a reasonable period of time to see if the student has made the connection to the recommended campus service or program. Here again, the relationship is key in using encouragement and advocacy to "glue" together various needs and services.

The Home

The stressors within the family can be part of the problem, and the strengths of the family can be part of the solution. Stressors might include housing, the development of employment-related skills, healthcare, respite, food and clothing deficiencies, the need for more education, etc. Strengths include those things that caregivers can do to support the student's learning, such as regular communication with the school, requiring daily or weekly progress reports, arranging for a time and place to do homework and reading, taking the student for a medical exam, participating in family therapy, spending more quality time with the student, implementing rewards and consequences, etc. The DPS or case manager may encounter a good deal of resistance on the part of the caregiver, and the worker will have to spend time trying to understand these obstacles and overcome them. Here again, the importance of the relationship cannot be overstated. This sort of teamwork effort can have a profoundly positive impact on the family's youngster; positive changes can and do occur.

> If you approach others with the thought of compassion, that will automatically reduce fear and allows for openness with other people. It creates a positive, friendly atmosphere. With that attitude, you can approach a relationship in which you, yourself, initially create the possibility of receiving a positive response from the other person. With that attitude, even if the other person is unfriendly or doesn't respond to you in a positive way, then at least you've approached the person with a feeling of openness that gives you flexibility, and the freedom to change your approach, as needed. That kind of openness at least allows the possibility of having a meaningful conversation with them.[1]

The Community

The DPS should have a good understanding of the range of services, agencies, providers, and programs available in the community. Most communities have service directories provided by United Way or other reputable umbrella organization. Some of the best ways to effect a referral to a particular service agency is to provide the caregiver with the name and phone number of a particular worker whom the DPS has built a relationship with or have the service provider meet with the DPS and family at the school in order to help make this important connection. I call this using the school as a "bridge." This approach is far more effective than simply passing on a name and phone number to parents or other team members. Again, this is where the personal relationship can have a significant impact in performing this role.

Team Roles

For the team to run smoothly, there are various roles that, as previously stated, can be shared. No role is never or always held by any one person. One suggestion is to rotate the roles at the end of each semester. The definitions of the various roles played by team members follow.

Facilitator

- Schedules meeting place, time, and date
- Ensures that meetings are held as scheduled
- Prepares the agenda that includes new referrals, follow-up on students previously discussed, and program coordination/development issues
- Begins and ends meetings on time
- Facilitates or moves the discussion along in a respectful way
- Ensures the agenda is covered in a timely manner
- Ensures that the administration and faculty are kept informed of care team activities

Recorder

- Creates and brings a record keeping system to each meeting, including the school calendar
- Keeps an attendance record of the core members of the care team
- Maintains records for all referrals
- Records salient information on the action plan document as the student is discussed
- Provides a verbal summary of decisions to ensure the accuracy of notes
- Notifies the facilitator of those students to be scheduled for a follow-up meeting

Timekeeper

- Assists the facilitator in starting and ending the meeting on time
- Keeps meeting on schedule once members have determined time allocations

Member(s)

- Arrive on time
- Notify facilitator if absence or lateness is anticipated

- Are prepared with relevant materials if presenting any part of the discussion about a particular student
- Help the group stay on focus
- Participate in "brainstorming" and provide suggestions and resources for every student discussed

Philosophy/Overview of the Student Success Team Process

The SST process is a problem-solving and coordinating approach that helps students, their families, teachers, and others to seek positive solutions for maximizing a student's potential. The SST philosophy is based on the belief that the school, home, and community need to work together to assist the student with obstacles that become evident in the school setting. The SST process seeks to set a course for assisting the student, build a network of support, implement a variety of interventions, and monitor the results.

Unlike a care team meeting, an SST always includes the student and his or her caregivers. It is very important for the student and caregiver to see that this meeting/ intervention planning process is not being done to them, but with them. They are full partners in the decisions that will be made collaboratively on behalf of our shared responsibility: the student. The criteria for holding an SST meeting is when it is felt that it would be useful to bring together the significant persons in the life of the student for an in-depth discussion of what issues are being manifest in school and to participate in SST intervention/action planning. The caregiver is encouraged to invite those individuals who can provide input and may be involved in the plan that is developed in the meeting. In addition to the student, caregiver(s), and support staff from the school, this might include a favorite aunt or uncle, a person to help interpret, a mentor, a mental health therapist, a religious person important to the student, a probation officer, etc. It is not uncommon to have four to seven people in addition to the student, caregivers, and school staff participate in the SST meeting.

Of course, a school SST can become overwhelmed by the number of students that school staff believe may benefit from this process, and this is a valid concern. One way to address this is for the school to have a sort of "filtering" process, or steps, that can come before first, before an SST is held. Such efforts may include having the student first discussed at teacher "family" meetings to strategize "classroom/teacher interventions" or having the school counselor meet with the student and caregiver first to see if a plan of assistance can be worked out. Nevertheless, it is not uncommon for a school to have 50 or more SSTs for new students in the school year and the same number of follow-up meetings.

In my experience, the SST process is particularly effective with attendance issues. The circle of communication is joined between all of the partners, and the student gets the clear message that these significant people in his or her life really want the best for him or her, both in school and in "real-life" and are in communication with each other.

You will find a number of forms and documents, including Frequently Asked Questions, to support the SST process in the Appendix. The SST Summary form is used to record the conversation as it moves along toward defining the actions/interventions that will be agreed upon. Many schools use a wall chart or white board to record the conversation live so that everyone can see what is being discussed. Typically, either the recorder or the facilitator of the meeting will stand in front of group that has gathered and, using a marking pen, list what is said under each column of the document. The wall chart is referred to as having a "header" and a "banner," the header being the list of items that go across the top of the page (Strengths, Known Information and Modifications Tried, Concerns, Strategies, Actions, Who, and When) and the banner being a piece of butcher paper that is taped below the header for the purposes of recording. Some schools have developed an approximate 6-foot header that is laminated to allow for repeated use. The banner is for one-time usage and can be kept as a record of the meeting in addition to the smaller version, a copy of which is given to everyone at the meeting. A black-board can also be used as the "banner." Some schools may use a computerized version of the wall chart that can be projected on a wall so that the meeting can be recorded in "real-time."

The SST Process and Assessment for Special Education and Section 504 Accommodations

A question that frequently comes up is the relationship between the SST process and referral for special education assessment. Although most school staffs prefer that various classroom and other interventions be tried prior to making a referral for consideration of special education eligibility assessment through the care team or through the SST process, this is not required if the student's parent/guardian (the person who holds educational rights) drafts a letter saying that they believe their youngster has an issue/condition that may qualify them for special education services and they are requesting an assessment. With regard to Section 504 eligibility, if the SST feels that the student may have an illness or disability that affects a major life function, they should refer the matter to the appropriate committee and provide any documentation to support the referral.

However, many of the issues that come before the SST have nothing to do with the possibility of an assessment for special education or 504 accommodations. Unfortunately, this truth is often neglected, and some staff believe that referring a student for an SST will be the vehicle to get a student into special education services or 504 accommodations. At times, one of the recommendations of the care team is for the student to have an "assessment," however, more often, again the Care team (SCCT) does not make such a recommendation. *The fact is that the SST process is neither a direct line to special education services or 504 accommodations or a roadblock to assessment for such services, nor should it be.*

Parents/Caregivers as Team Members

Being a parent of a youngster who is having difficulties in school, at home, and/or in the community is very stressful. It is easy to feel guilty and to blame one's self for what is occurring. Often parents fear that the "school people" will blame them, make them shoulder the full burden of responsibility, and won't be supportive. These parents may have a history of having been involved in meetings with other school officials, meetings that may have been painful or where they felt devalued. They may have shared their story and concerns with other school personnel in the past, but, due to the lack of articulation between schools and levels, this information was not "passed along," and they are hesitant to start over with new people. Previous meetings may have been less than collaborative, with information and perceptions presented to them by "professionals," with little regard for their input or perspective.

We DPSs may know that the SST process is collaborative, not into blaming, and may be more positive than any other meeting parents have ever attended at a school. But parents do not know this. So we must help them to understand how this process honors them and that we want to join with them on behalf of their youngster. Our challenge as educators is to create honest, open, two-way communication, cooperation, and collaboration between the important adults in the home life of the youngster and the significant adults in the school.

School success cannot be achieved by any of the parties working in isolation. As school staff, we cannot be successful without the involvement of the family, just as they cannot guarantee school success without our involvement.

Outreach to the family and preparation for the meeting is crucial. The SST brochure is a good overview for families, but it cannot take the place of personal contact, encouragement, and assistance when needed. In preparing a parent/caregiver for participation in the SST process, we must be sensitive to their issues while believing that we have it within our power to calm their concerns, to reassure them that we have the best interests of their child at heart, and to prepare them for a meeting that will focus on joining together those individuals and resources that can lead to success for their youngster. It must be clear to everyone that the caregiver(s) is an equal member of the team in the development of a plan for success.

A Brief Note About the Absent Parent, Most Often the Father

Many schools accept a statement from the custodial parent that the absent parent is "out of the picture," and the school should/will only deal with them, the custodial parent. I believe this is a mistake because the absence of one of the parents may be one of the main underlying reasons for the student's alienation from the school, depression, acting out, or dropping out. If the absent parent is anywhere in the geographical area, I believe it is a worthwhile effort to reach out to this parent and let them know how important it is to the school that they become involved in their child's education and, by extension, their life as well. Even if there is "bad blood" between the biological parents, they can hopefully understand that their youngster needs both parents to be involved if they are to be successful, and it may be helpful to explain the potential negative implications if they continue not to be involved.

What Do Parents Really Want from the School and Its Personnel?

First and foremost, the caregiver(s) want to know that you, as a representative of the school, have the best interest of their child at heart and that you truly want to join with them for the benefit of their child. It has been my experience that if the caregivers believe that their child is really cared about, this can transcend any racial, ethnic, or language barriers that may be present. They also want to know that you are a person of integrity, but they will not be able to determine that until after you have worked together and they see that you are a person who follows through on your commitments and does not disappoint them.

Tips on Outreach to Parents/Caregivers

1. Reaching out to and engaging the parent(s)/caregiver(s) is a key element in making the SST process successful. This effort is much more than sending a written notice of a meeting or making a phone call. It involves extending oneself as a representative of the school and serving as a "bridge" for the parent to enter the school environment.

2. The person who performs the outreach/engagement role must be sensitive to the issues that may cause the caregiver to "resist" meeting with the school. Information about the purpose of the meeting must be presented with an emphasis on shared concerns and responsibilities. The parent must be given an opportunity to ask any questions or share any concerns they may have with the upcoming meeting.

3. Keep in mind that, as a representative of the school or district, you may be seen more of a symbol of an uncaring system than who you really are. Caregivers may have had bad experiences in the past with school personnel, and they may initially think that you will be the same way. Only with your compassionate approach can that negative history change to that of an open and receptive partner.

4. Parents/caregivers may also have time, work, childcare, or transportation issues which can complicate their ability to participate in the meeting. The SST process must include support for parents to accommodate these very real issues. Any support provided has both symbolic and concrete meaning to parents and contributes to the success of the meeting for the caregivers, other team members, and the student.

Put Yourself in the "Shoes" of Another: Home Visiting Tips

If you have reached out to the caregiver either through a phone call or a mailing but have not been able to connect, it may be time to consider a home visit. It may be that, in addition to academic issues, there may be other specific concerns, and we would like to get a better understanding of the environment the student is living in. We are all aware that there are some neighborhoods that are less than safe, and each person will have to think about the risks and potential benefits of making a venture to a student's home. One rule of thumb is not to go alone but to join with another member of the student support team. A male/female team is great if those personnel are part of the team.

I recall one home visit where we found the family literally loading their possessions into a truck because they had been evicted. Being knowledgeable about some community resources that the family apparently did not know about, we jumped on our phones and went to work. Within an hour we were able to obtain enough funding to reverse the eviction, giving the family a little more time to get their finances together. They were so happy about what we were able to do to keep a roof over their heads, working with them from that point forward was a real teamwork effort. In each instance our goal is to develop a "working alliance" with the members of the students' home.

Once inside the residence—or standing outside the door, if the caregiver is hesitant to allow you in—state clearly your concerns about their youths' poor attendance and tell them you would like to work with them to improve the situation. Give them an opportunity to ask questions, to share their views on the causes of the truancy or other concerns, and listen to what they believe might help.

Before going out to the home, consider any cultural and/or language issues that may present a barrier if you are not prepared. In some families, the primary person to relate to is the mother; in others, it will be the father or other important people who are part of the extended family.

- If refreshment is offered, accept it. In many cultures it is perceived as an insult not to accept such an offer. The "breaking of bread" has an important symbolic meaning.
- Be prepared to answer questions that they may have of you in the initial part of the interview. Don't be defensive, even if a personal question is asked, such as "do you have children?". Attempts to "check you out" are generally made to determine if you can be trusted with their very personal insights and information. Even if their questions seem somewhat hostile, try not to be personally offended. A negative attitude may reflect previous bad experiences with educators and agencies, or reflect the general frustration of trying to cope with the child's difficulty. Allow for or encourage the caregiver(s) need to ventilate if you perceive it may be necessary. It may be difficult for them to start working again with a new person or team from the school, particularly if there has been a lack of articulation and continuity with others they may have worked with previously. This ventilation may be necessary prior to effectively moving on to other issues.

Throughout our work with parent(s)/guardians, we are always trying to strengthen the natural relationship between parent and child. We are willing to share the "burden" with them, but allowing too many of the responsibilities to shift to us will only weaken the alliance we are trying to enhance.

Those schools that maintain regular and ongoing communication with the homes of the students have a much better chance of keeping their youth on track, and this communication lessens the chances that the student will eventually drop out.

Including the Student in the SST Meeting: The Powerful Message

It is useful if a member of the team can meet with the student prior to the actual SST meeting to answer questions they may have about the purpose and process of the meeting. During this orientation meeting, the student may be asked to complete a brief, open-ended questionnaire about his or her likes and dislikes regarding school, their future goals, and what they would like the outcome of the meeting to be. When the purpose of the meeting is explained and they hear that they are an equal member of the team and that their input is welcomed and needed, most respond positively.

Coming unprepared into a room with a number of adults can be very uncomfortable. When the student enters the room and sees the important adults in his or her life, a powerful message of caring and commitment to their success is given. By virtue of the fact that adults have busy schedules and yet they have all found a way to come together on their behalf, the importance of the occasion and the potential importance of the student's future is evident. Make no mistake: the student clearly gets this powerful message, even if they are not overjoyed at the onset of what some may perceive as "facing the music." Only by joining with all of the parties in a solution-oriented process toward success can we hope to achieve positive change.

As has been stated, an SST meeting always starts with each person gathered sharing what they see as the student's strengths. Through this process, the student hears that while there will be a discussion of the problems *of* the student, she or he is not *the* problem. The powerful effect of hearing his or her strengths listed by these significant adults for her or his self-image cannot be overestimated. Involving the student in decisions that affect his or her life empowers them and often helps to gain their cooperation in assuming responsibilities for some of the action items.

Involving the Younger Child

Once I attended an SST meeting for a 1st-grade student. The student was not asked to join the meeting because members of the team thought he was too young. During the meeting there was a small noise coming from under the table in the library where the meeting was being held. It was, of course, the boy, who knew that a meeting was being held about him and that his parents/caregivers were there, and he simply wanted to find out what was going on. It is not hard to understand that a child may become anxious about the meeting and wonder what the outcome might be.

An easy way to demystify the meeting and the child's worry about it is to invite the child to attend. Even the youngest child is able to share what he or she likes and dislikes about school, and they may be able to share their ideas about what might make school more successful for them.

At the caregiver's discretion, younger children may be asked to step outside or go back to their classroom for part of the meeting while the caregiver shares sensitive information that they would prefer the child not be present for. Another option for handling sensitive information would be to schedule another meeting between the caregiver and a member of the SST. This separate meeting can be listed as an item on the action plan. The sensitivity as to how long the child should stay in the meeting is left up to the facilitator and the caregiver to determine. In any case, every child should be present for the recitation of the student's strengths because of its obvious positive effect on the student. Helping the child to feel comfortable in the meeting is a first step to their feeling comfortable with working with adults on a school success plan.

It is unfortunate but true that poor school attendance starts early, and many younger children are already setting the stage to become dropouts as early as the 2nd or 3rd grade, and sometimes even earlier, especially if they are having trouble learning to read.

With many young children, there may be complicity on the part of the parents/caregivers that contributes to the attendance/truancy problem. I recall being sent to a kindergarten class on the first day of school to assist the teacher with starting the year smoothly. Many children were crying and looking at their parents as if to say "please don't leave me." It appeared that many of the parents were having a harder time leaving the child than the child leaving the parent. At times, there are subtle or not so subtle messages going to the child that the parent needs them or would like to have them to stay at home. At times the caregiver may have a genuine medical problem, and they may need some assistance at home, but to put that responsibility on a child is very unfair. I have seen children who think that their parent/caregiver may die while they are away at school, and they feel they need to stay close to home to avoid such an unfortunate happening. These are just a few of the many reasons that can contribute to early and serious attendance problems, and they underline why it is so important to understand the root causes of the problem and develop a plan of assistance before it is literally too late.

Some Tips to Make the Student Success Team More Successful

- It is important to designate core members of the team in addition to the occasional members who will differ for each student. The core members include the facilitator/chairperson and the recorder. These roles are fluid and can change from meeting to meeting or for a defined period of time.
- After everyone has been introduced, it is very important to start the meeting's discussion with the first column on the left side of the SST Summary chart, a description of *student strengths*. This sets a positive tone for the meeting and gives everyone an opportunity to be heard, thus setting the stage for equal input and respectful listening.
- A broad range of interventions should be considered, including the classroom, the larger school environment, the home, and the community.
- Action items should be selected from the "brainstorming" activity, with follow-up responsibilities being assigned to as many participants as possible, a timeline defined, and a follow-up meeting scheduled.
- Make sure that all participants sign the bottom of the summary form to verify their attendance, as well as to give their agreement to the interventions/actions decided upon to move forward.
- Determine a "point person," often referred to as a "case manager" (I prefer *care coordinator* or DPS to case manager) to ensure that the plan gets "glued together." *If the action items are not implemented, the plan will most likely fail.*

Facilitation of the SST Process

How the SST meeting is facilitated, or how any meeting at the school is facilitated, is crucial to its outcome. Most of us were not trained in this skill. It will take practice and involves taking risks in this role. People will look to the facilitator to "set the stage" and make everyone comfortable by making sure that everyone has a chance to introduce him- or herself and describe his or her relationship to the student (i.e., "I am the school nurse"). Once again, the facilitator should explain the purpose and process of the meeting, especially to the student and their caregiver. Facilitation is a way of providing leadership without taking the reins. Your job is to facilitate, to get others to put forth their thoughts and ideas and assume some responsibility for being part of the "solution." So, what are the core components of being a facilitator?

- The facilitator should make the necessary arrangements for the meeting: all participants are notified as to time and place, roles are defined in advance, all relevant material for the meeting is obtained, and the SST summary is posted on the wall.
- The facilitator should guide the meeting along, being mindful of the time, the importance of covering each column topic, and keeping the tone positive.
- Stay neutral on content: focus on the process. This doesn't mean that you can't offer suggestions; it just means that you shouldn't impose your opinions on the topic before the group.
- Listen actively: look people in the eye, use positive body language.
- Ask questions, test assumptions, invite participation, and gather information.
- Paraphrase to clarify, such as "Are you saying . . . ?," "What I'm hearing you say is. . . ."
- Synthesize ideas. Get people to comment on what others are saying and build on their thoughts.
- The SST Summary chart/document serves as a visual record of the discussion and the actions/interventions that are decided upon.
- Stay on track: set a time line for the meeting and appoint a timekeeper. Use a "parking lot" to record ideas that are important but not on topic.
- Give and receive feedback. Ask members how they feel the meeting is going or if you are making progress. Regularly evaluate the effectiveness of the process.
- Bring assumptions out into the open, clarify them, and challenge them, if indicated.
- Collect ideas: keep track of emerging ideas and final decisions. Notes should reflect what people actually said and not your interpretation of what was said.
- Summarize to revive a discussion that has come to a halt or to end a discussion when things seem to be wrapping up.
- Identify action items, who is responsible, and when tasks are to be accomplished.

(See the SST Facilitator Observation Checklist in the Appendix.)

School Attendance Review Team

Every school should have a SART to follow the progress of students whose attendance patterns are of concern. Most high school districts have scan forms that teachers mark to indicate whether a student is present or absent from their class. Most primary and elementary schools keep track of daily attendance on forms that are entered on the district's mainframe computer, much like the secondary schools scan forms. As stated in Chapter 1, this is important because the district mainframe can print out period-by-period attendance for secondary students, and a daily, weekly, or monthly attendance record for younger children. Via the tech department, each school can be sent a list of students who are missing school by their name, grade, counselor of record, and the percent of time the student is absent, either excused or unexcused. What is important is how the school uses this information. Typically, this is the job of the SART. The SART is usually made up of some or all of the following: school counselor(s), school social worker, dean or head counselor, DPS, parent liaison, an attendance worker, a special education representative, teacher(s) of the student, school resource officer, and a probation officer if one is assigned to the school to monitor the student(s) on their caseload.

It is useful for the SART to develop a grid or spreadsheet to track the various efforts/interventions made to address the truancy pattern of each student whom they are monitoring. Items on the spreadsheet may include notification letter(s) sent to the home, phone calls to the caregiver(s), meetings with the student and caregiver with a contract developed, home visits, SST meetings held, class schedule changes, tutorial assistance offered, referrals to a community-based or city agency, or possibly a referral to the district/city student attendance review board.

Much like the care team and the SST, the SART works to uncover ("peeling the onion") the underlying problem that is manifest and works to address the issues that are identified using any and all of the resources they have at their disposal. It is far too easy, at least in most large high schools and some large middle schools, for a student to float along under the radar until they literally have a foot out the door—which is soon to be both feet out the door. This is why it is very important that members of the SART search the list of absent students and develop a list of those whose attendance issues should be addressed.

Just like the Care team, the SART works to identify patterns of systemic issues that may be contributing to poor attendance and dropouts in the school/district and, additionally, puts preventative attendance practices and programs in place.

School Attendance Review Board

When the SART has done its "due diligence" and can document what they have done to address the issues of a particular student without success, they may decide to refer the matter to the district/city structure called the *school attendance review board* (SARB).

In addition to the important district staff that make up the Board, including representative(s) from the referring school, it is useful for the SARB to involve a staff member from various community-based or public agencies who may be able to provide needed services to the student and his or her family. This may include representatives from county/community mental health, social services, the juvenile probation department, the District Attorney's (DA) office (if your city has a "truancy court calendar"), and others who may be able to deliver needed services.

The SARB is a somewhat more formal structure and process than the SART because this will often be the "last stop" before referring the student to the DA for the matter to be scheduled before a judge who oversees the Truancy Court. It is important for both the student and his or her caregivers to understand that serious consequences may come into play if the student's attendance does not improve, such as a fine, community service, suspension of the students drivers license, etc.

Most often a certified formal letter is sent to the caregiver with a return signature receipt attached so that it is clear that this is "serious business" and that they are expected to attend the hearing. However, much like other meetings at/with the school, a letter alone does not ensure the attendance of the caregiver. It is important that a member of the SARB reach out to the caregiver and discuss with them any barriers that may keep them from attending. Such issues as the need for childcare, lack of transportation, no money for bus fare, and work commitments may be some of the reasons given as to why they may not be able to attend the hearing. The DPS/SARB worker should do his or her best to address these barriers with the caregiver. These may include having someone in the district providing childcare for a young child, picking up the caregiver and driving them to the meeting, writing a letter to their employer describing the importance of their worker attending this meeting, etc. In any case, the SARB worker has to "think out of the box" in helping the caregiver address those barriers that may be present to determine whether or not the caregiver(s) can attend the SARB hearing.

A member of the SARB must be designated to receive the referrals of students to the SARB, to critique the referral for completeness, and to make the necessary arrangements for the hearing to take place. Most districts have developed a form that includes the information expected/required for the school site SART to refer the matter to the SARB. This referral packet should include, but not be limited to, a teacher input form from each teacher of the student; documentation of the efforts the school-site SART has undertaken; copies of important documents such as the student's transcript, attendance history, and grades in progress; copies of SST and follow-up meeting(s), etc. If the referral packet is not complete, the SARB worker should send it back to the school for more complete information. This will not only be beneficial for this one student, but will let the school-site SART know what is expected for the referral of students yet to come.

The SARB worker should also discuss with the caregiver and the student if there are other significant people or program representatives who should be invited to the hearing. These might include a mental health therapist, probation officer, favorite uncle or aunt, a mentor of the student, or possibly an interpreter if one is needed.

Most SARB hearings can be held and concluded in about 45 minutes, followed by a debriefing of the just completed hearing and a brief background and overview of the next student to come before the SARB. Therefore, the SARB agenda should schedule each student for about 1 complete hour, although some flexibility should exist based on circumstances.

The flow of the meeting can follow a sort of "script" as follows:

1. Start with introductions of every person in the room. Ask each person to state their name and what their role is in relation to this matter. It is also a good idea for each person, as they introduce themselves, to state something positive or a strength they see in this student (4–5 minutes). It is important to keep in mind that the student is not the problem, but that he or she is having a problem with attending school on a regular basis. An old friend of mine once said, "The problem is the problem; the student is not the problem."
2. The SARB chair should explain the purpose of the hearing and the hope for a positive outcome for the student, the caregiver(s), and for the school district. The chairperson should also inform the student and caregiver of the legal responsibility for the student to attend school and that the possibility of more serious consequences does exist (3–4 minutes).

3. If a representative of the DA's office is in attendance, the DA representative should be given an opportunity to present the possible involvement of the courts both verbally and in writing (if he or she has a handout that states legal mandates and possible consequences (3–4 minutes).

4. Ask the school representative to provide an explanation of the reason for the referral, what the school site has tried to do to resolve the attendance issue, and how their efforts have been successful or unsuccessful (4–5 minutes).

5. Ask the student to share from their perspective what the issue is that is causing them to miss so much school. Ask the student what they need and what would be helpful to them to assist them in attending school more regularly. Ask what they can do to improve the situation. Ask what the school can do to improve the situation (4–5 minutes).

6. Provide an opportunity for those gathered around the table to ask questions of the student, the caregiver(s), and the other important people in the student's life (6–8 minutes).

7. Ask each person gathered around the table for a suggestion on how to address the truancy situation (brainstorming) (4–5 minutes).

8. Develop an action plan from the brainstormed ideas, including who is responsible for each action and When each action/intervention is to occur. The SARB should consider, much like the care team and the SST, the broad range of interventions available in the classroom, the larger school environment, the home, and the community (8–10 minutes).

9. Ask if anyone has any questions that have not been answered, or if they need any further clarification of the process.

10. The chairperson should conclude the meeting by thanking everyone for attending and expressing the hope that the discussion and action items identified will be helpful in improving the truancy and bring school success for the student.

Questions to think about:

1. Understand that the school's first task is to develop a system in which students experiencing difficulties are identified, early interventions or modifications are attempted, and, if unsuccessful, a more thorough examination will occur. How does this occur at your school?

2. What role do you see yourself playing on each of these teams (SCCT, SST, SART, SARB)?
3. Is the early identification and intervention system well defined and known to all staff?
4. What can you do to initiate and institutionalize an early identification and intervention process in your school if the current process is lacking?
5. The school needs to designate a person or persons to receive and screen requests for services and to schedule students for discussion before the appropriate team. Who is that person at your school?
6. If you were a parent or guardian attending a meeting at the school, such as an SST meeting, what would be important to you regarding how you were approached and treated?
7. Does your district/city have a SARB? What can you do to bring about this structure in your district if one is currently lacking?

4

Case Management
A Creative Philosophy and Form of Practice

It is true that those interventions/actions decided in good faith by the school coordinated care team (SCCT), the student success team (SST), or the school attendance review team (SART) are only as good as the follow-up that ensures that the strategies agreed to in the meetings are implemented. Nevertheless, many people confuse follow-up with the often used term "case management." In fact, the practice of case management starts much earlier in the seven (7) step process, and that process will be the focus of this chapter. Let's take a look at a fuller description of this process often called *case management*.

The Problem That Case Management Seeks to Address

The problems of our current service delivery system include services that are crisis-oriented and that lack an emphasis on prevention, services that divide the problems of children and families into distinct categories that fail to reflect interrelated causes and solutions, a lack of communication and collaboration among the various public and private agencies, and the inability of specialized agencies to easily craft comprehensive solutions to complex problems. There is a need to improve the coordination and integration of efforts within the school and school system, and these can also be factors that contribute to dysfunction.

Why Schools?

Schools remain the one institution of society that is in the forefront. All of the problems and issues of the society are manifested in the schools because children bring these issues with them when they enter the schoolhouse door. Our schools are literally the magnifying glass of our society. We, who work in

The Dropout Prevention Specialist Workbook. Howard M. Blonsky, Oxford University Press (2020).
© Oxford University Press.
DOI: 10.1093/oso/9780190090845.003.0008

and with schools, find ourselves in a unique position to design, implement, and monitor those comprehensive service plans tailored to address a student's needs. Schools are the natural place where children's needs and resources can be joined.

Although case management was not initially a function of education, we know that a child's education can be enhanced by addressing the social, health, psychological, and other issues that may be affecting their ability to progress. Therefore, it is important that a member of the care team, the SST, or the SART, be it a dropout prevention specialist (DPS), a school social worker, a counselor, a nurse, or another member of the team, assume the role of care/case manager, whether they are called by that name or not.

Is the Term "Case Management" a User Friendly Term?

Although the term "case management" is used in a variety of settings by individuals from different disciplines and is sometimes used by untrained personnel who hook onto this much too often used term, it is not a term that truly reflects either the philosophy or form of this practice. To some, the term "case management" implies that those who are "case managers" are "controlling" or "managing" their clients and doing the work for them. We must be careful not to use this term with our clients because it can sound derogatory to them. If someone says to a client, "I am your case manager," the client may be well within their rights to say, "I am not a case, and I don't need to be managed," and who could blame them for that kind of retort? In reality, what is called case management is actually *an empowerment philosophy and form of practice* where the care/case manager works in collaboration with clients to develop and implement a package of services that best addresses their needs. The package of services should include those provided directly by the case manager, the school, and the school district through its range of opportunities, services, and supports, as well as those from city and/or community agencies.

Some terms that may be more appropriate than case management are "care coordination," "client-centered comprehensive services development and implementation," and "service coordination." However, because the term "case management" is so commonly used, it will be used in this discussion as well. But remember not to use with your clients (students and caregivers) because of the negative connotation that it implies.

The Importance of the Relationship

The case management process depends on the unique relationship between the student/family and the care or case manager. The relationship is the heart of the process. This is a relationship based on trust, and the importance of that relationship cannot be overstated. The care/case manager literally provides the "glue" that helps to keep the plan together and provides continuity over time, which is necessary to bring the goals and actions that have been agreed upon to full implementation. The case manager is always working to empower the client to do as much for him- or herself as possible but is flexible enough to "pick up the ball" when that seems necessary. The case manager does not want to do too much or too little and literally walks a sort of tightrope in making sure that the package of services actually comes together.

The Case Manager: A Definition

The case manager is the primary person who, through his or her personal relationship with the student and family, provides the foundation for motivation and support in providing, coordinating, advocating for, and maintaining the network of services and resources necessary to maintain academic and social progress. The case manager and his or her client(s) work together to define and develop a package of services that are comprehensive, flexible, client-centered, coordinated, goal-oriented, and, therefore, more effective.

The goal of the case manager is to empower each of the participants in the plan to follow through on the responsibilities they assumed in the service/action planning phase and to do so in a timely manner. The case manager has to walk a fine line as to when or whether he or she takes a more active role in working to ensure that the action items are put into place. At times this may require encouragement, advocacy, and/or monitoring or, in some instances, "taking the bull by the horns" to "glue" together the various action items.

Keep in mind that the "case manager" is the *primary provider* of the service plan. Other programs and resources are mobilized when there are things that the case manager cannot do by him- or herself.

Case Management: A Definition

Case management is a method of providing services whereby the case manager in collaboration with other members of the school service team and along with the student and his or her family determine appropriate strategies and actions to address the needs of a student. When appropriate, the case manager arranges, provides, advocates for, coordinates, monitors, and evaluates the overall implementation of the plan. The goal is to develop and implement a package of services that is comprehensive, culturally appropriate, and coherent, and to do so in a caring way.

While all of the words encompassed in this definition are important, *coordination and connectedness* are probably the keys. For if the plan for the student/family is not coordinated, and if the connections stated in the service/action plan do not happen, the plan will most likely fail.

The Steps in the Case Management Process

Step 1: Identification and Outreach

Many times those who are most in need do not seek out services on their own or do not know how to go about getting them. Often, access is not user friendly or the motivation is not sufficient to get through the hoops necessary to obtain the services needed. Students show their needs in the school setting, either through their grades, attendance, visits to the school nurse with undefined complaints, disciplinary and behavior problems, revealing papers written and turned into teachers, and, at times, a direct request to a staff member. If we pay attention to these warning signs, we can easily identify those students who may benefit from case management services and, by extension, their families. As I said, these young people may not be asking for services, but they may be the perfect ones to receive case management services. Within the dropout-prone population, the signs are everywhere that a particular student may be a candidate for case management services.

"Outreach" refers to utilizing the resources of the school and/or district to find the student/client and make some initial contact. If they are still attending school, this should not be too much of a problem. However, if they are no longer attending, it may involve venturing out into the community to locate them, going to the last known address, and, if the student is not there, speaking to neighbors or other youth to try to get some clues regarding how to locate them.

Step 2: Engagement

This is the most crucial step in the process. If a relationship of trust is not developed between the case manager and the student, along with his or her

---

family, there is very little chance that any plan of service will be successful. There is no set number of meetings that are required, but the case manager must give the student/family a sense that their interest in them is genuine and that they have the intention to stick with them for a significant period of time. As previously stated, this relationship will serve as the basis for the motivation to keep the plan moving forward and to make sure that it is implemented. The case manager must impart to the student/family that she is a person of integrity and that she will follow-through with her end of the "bargain."

Step 3: Intake and Assessment

The case manager (or DPS) has to get to know the student and the family composition in which the student lives. This includes gaining the perspective of the student and family on the issues their youngster is facing, including possible interrelationships and origins. Case managers often carry with them a "case file," with forms, questionnaires, and tracking information. Some feel they must complete everything within this document at the first meeting, but I would recommend against this practice. By putting yourself in the same situation, it is easy to understand why someone would not feel comfortable facing a barrage of questions. Immigrant caregivers may suspect that the information presented may be used with the Immigration and Naturalization Service (INS) and lead to bigger problems for them. The case manager does want to learn the answers to all of the questions, but this can only be done in the process of spending time with the student and family. As they come to trust the case manager more, additional information will be revealed. It is best if the case manager keeps the questions in mind as he or she talks with the various parties and then enters the answers into the case file after the direct contact is completed. Of course, documents such as permissions, requests to exchange information, and others forms may need to be completed at the first meeting. Only by thoroughly getting to know the various sources of information will it be possible to collaboratively craft a service/action/care plan.

Step 4: Development of the Service/Action/Care Plan

Until the case manager has a good idea of the issues, their possible interrelationships, and origins, he or she will be unable to develop a service plan of action in partnership with the student/family. Once the case manager has a good sense of the areas to be addressed, he or she works in partnership with the student/family to define the plan that will be put into action. I cannot emphasize enough the importance of collaboratively developing the plan: we develop the plan "with them" not "to them." This is consistent with the philosophy of case management as an empowerment form of practice. The more that clients can define their own goals and the issues that they see a need to address, the better, and the less to do for the case manager. It is important that the responsibilities are shared and that no one person is burdened with too many of the responsibilities. By undertaking some of the responsibilities for the actions to be implemented, the case manager imparts that she is a member of the team.

Step 5: Implementation of the Plan

With close attention to the "who" and the "when," efforts to implement the plan get started. Yes, this may seem like a long way from Step 1, but again, this is a process that follows defined steps. The case manager should let the others who have assumed responsibilities know that they can come to him or her with any questions or difficulties they may be having in bringing the plan to fruition.

Step 6: Monitoring and Modification When Needed

It is very important to monitor the "benchmarks" and other indicators that the service plan has been put into effect. It is also important to obtain feedback from the student/family on how things are going and whether the implemented opportunities, services, and supports are being helpful. At times it is necessary to modify the service/care plan for one reason or another. Therefore, the case manager needs to maintain regular communication with the student/family and maintain a willingness to help in whatever way is necessary to bring about success.

Step 7: Evaluation

It goes without saying that evaluation is more important today than ever. Every funding source, grant, etc. wants to see outcome data. When serving humans, qualitative data are just as important as quantitative data. Therefore, changes that are perceived by the student him- or herself, teachers, family members, and others are just as important as those things that can be measured. It might be useful to mark items in the case file that will be part of the evaluation process to make sure that they are not forgotten.

Core Principles of Case Management

1. *Case management requires partnership.*

   Case management is first and foremost a system of partnerships: between case manager and client, and between organizations. In an effective case management process, the case manager works in partnership "with" the client, sharing responsibility, rather than working "on" the client.

2. *Case management communicates respect for the client.*

   The success of any case management effort depends on the degree to which the young person is engaged in the development and joint ownership of the service/care plan and has a major stake in ensuring its success. In every aspect, the client has to be treated as a mature, responsible person, not as a number or a child.

3. *Case management must provide predictability.*

   Many disadvantaged youth experience life as a series of random events over which they have little control. Successful case management works to rebuild a sense of control and predictability by helping young people to plan, set goals, and undertake helping efforts on their own behalf.

Qualifications for Case Managers

Disciplined Empathy

Effective case managers seem to exhibit what might be called "disciplined empathy." They respect and care about their clients, and they can develop a partnerships with them. They listen to what clients say, read between the lines, and paraphrase what they have heard back to the student/family member. Case managers have a compassionate but tough-minded understanding of the youth they work with; they have the ability to develop a "therapeutic" alliance and to challenge and confront youth to meet their end of the responsibilities when indicated

Partnership Skills

At the same time, case managers have the skills to develop partnerships with both individuals and institutions. Diplomatic sensitivity is a key trait. Case managers need to adopt a philosophy that any blocks to client self-determination are both internal and external and constantly interact. Efforts to help must aim at changing both the individual and the environment.

Empowerment

Case managers need the ability to help students/families develop and effectively utilize their own internal problem-solving and coping resources.

Case Management: Key Concepts

1. "Service coordination" or "care coordination" is a more user-friendly term for the process referred to by many as "case management."
2. Our schools are in a unique position to address the needs of the whole child and his or her family.
3. Our schools are the great magnifying glass of society. The students bring their issues with them to school on a daily basis, and all things can come to light in the school setting.
4. The trusting relationship between the case manager, the student, and his or her family is the heart of the process. Therefore, the relationship serves as the "glue" that holds the plan together.
5. The care/case management relationship empowers the student and family by joining with them in a plan of success.
6. The case manager conveys the belief to students/caregivers that they have the power to improve their situations.
7. The ownership of the service/care plan by the student/family is a significant factor in whether the efforts/action items planned will be effective.
8. It is important for the care/case manager to empower the student/family and, when appropriate, have the willingness to take a more active role to ensure the action items are put into place. It is sort of like walking a tightrope: not doing too much or too little, always adjusting the balance based on the circumstances.
9. The care/case manager should be familiar with the range of interventions and resources that can be utilized in the classroom, the larger school environment, the home, and the community (the "broad" range of interventions).
10. Developing a personal relationship with service providers from various agencies can help to bridge students and families to those services that are not provided directly by the care/case manager.

Questions to think about:

1. Are case management services provided in your school?
2. Do you feel you have the skills and personal attributes to serve as a care/case manager? What are they? Are there others on your team who can share in these responsibilities?
3. Is there anything you can do to bring to a case management process to your school for students with serious truancy problems?

5

School Climate and Culture and Its Relationship to Dropout Prevention

A certain measurement of school climate is whether students are attending school or not.[1]

School climate is a pervasive thing. Most educators have experienced the positive and negative effects of it. It's possible to get a good feel for it within the first five minutes of entering the school. Students send powerful messages through their facial expressions and body language. It's often possible to tell whether they are busy, noisy, silent, engaged, or bored with just a glance. Look at the state of the playground, parking lot, and school buildings. Are they clean or unkempt? Walk past students and staff, and notice how they watch, look at, greet, or stare at you. Are you welcomed or ignored when you enter the building? Look around at the walls to see how are they decorated? Open your ears and listen to what you hear in the hallways. Depending on the school, they may be filled with positive interactions among students and adults or the harsh sounds of adults chastising and hushing students walking between classes.

The truth is that every school has a climate. It is either developed—planned with intent—or it is adopted by proxy. When planned with positive intent, it can be supportive, protective, nurturing, and conducive to effective teaching and learning. Unfortunately, when neglected, it can also be unsafe, unsupportive, and disconnected. Imagine that you are a teacher, or parent entering such a school on a daily or weekly basis. How would it make you feel, motivated or distracted, supported or vulnerable?[2]

The Dropout Prevention Specialist Workbook. Howard M. Blonsky, Oxford University Press (2020).
© Oxford University Press.
DOI: 10.1093/oso/9780190090845.003.0008

Whenever I have graduate students preparing to become school social workers, I ask them to put themselves in the shoes of a student enrolled in their assigned school and see how the environment/climate feels to them. As the "student," do people acknowledge you and say "good morning"? Are there bulletin boards that celebrate diversity and recognize student achievements? Is the building clean and inviting? Do the teachers greet students at the door of their classrooms, shake their hands, and invite them in? Is there a posted listing of opportunities, such as clubs and other activities for students to participate in? Do the teachers seem generally happy to be teaching at this school? Are the rules and expectations for students clearly stated and visible? Do the disciplinary practices seem fair and evenly enforced? These are some of the signs to look for in evaluating the culture and climate of the school.

Let's take a look at some significant negative (toxic) school climate indicators as listed by Ramsey.

- A blend of negative expectations and pessimism regarding students
- An attitude that there is nothing wrong with the school; there is merely an influx of inferior students
- A philosophy of discipline based on fear, intimidation, coercion, and punishment
- A blatant disregard for student rights
- A larger measure of inattention and insensitivity to ethnic or racial concerns
- An absence of any student involvement and input in any significant decision-making process
- A rigid, unrealistic, and sometimes punitive grading policy
- A reward system that recognizes only a very narrow number of successes
- A drab physical environment[3]

> How do you know when a school is toxic? One can walk into a toxic school and see the dirt on the floor, the graffiti on the walls or smell coming from the student bathrooms. Thankfully, the percentage of schools that are truly toxic is small. However, many schools have practices that exhibit one of the following four properties: toxicity to student learning, toxicity to students, toxicity to parents and toxicity to staff.

The Dropout Prevention Specialist Workbook

Toxicity to Students

- Bullying is ignored rather than being prevented, and bullies are not punished.
- Although the school professes to treat all students equally, athletes or members of the student government are given "privileges" that are denied to the bulk of the student population. *Inequitable and unfair dispensation of discipline is consistently cited by dropouts as a primary reason they decided to leave school.*
- Students ditch classes with regularity while the school ignores the behavior or looks for the causes.
- Failure of classes and examinations is ignored, and the school does not identify the causes of failure.[4]

Some schools do not have a nurturing environment for both staff and students. These schools are often referred to as "toxic." A quote from a staff member in one of them follows:

> We had a poor curriculum, poor student–staff relationships, and no sense of "community togetherness." Most students did not feel like we were a family. For the sake of the students we had to design a process for encouraging relationships of trust between students and staff. Students have difficulty learning until they connect with staff. (School for Integrated Academics and Technologies, Los Angeles Unified School District)[5]
>
> School culture is like the air we breathe; you don't really notice it until it becomes toxic.[6]

Box 5.1 is a School Climate Profile that can be used at your school site and/or district and adapted as indicated. I recall doing a professional development workshop at a county office of education. At one point we took out this profile and asked the staff to complete it. The Superintendent, who was standing close by, thought the exercise was foolish because he was sure that all of the responses would be the most positive possible. He was certainly surprised when that turned out not to be the case. You might consider having the staff and faculty at your school take this survey/profile: see what comes up and what can be learned from this exercise.

Resiliency and School Climate

Unfortunately I have often heard school staff make comments such as "What do you expect us to do? This child comes from a broken home, from a poor

Box 5.1 School Climate Profile

The following questions should be rated on a scale of 1 to 5, with 1 = Almost Never, 2 = Occasionally, 3 = Frequently, 4 = Almost Always, 5 = Always.

1. Students are treated with respect by teachers.
2. Students can count on teachers to listen to their side of the story and to be fair.
3. Students feel enthusiastic about learning in this school and enjoy coming to school.
4. Staff enjoys working in this school.
5. I feel that my ideas will be listened to in this school.
6. Parents are considered by this school as important contributors.
7. Staff at this school are continually seeking ways to improve the educational program.
8. The school program is appropriate to students' present and future needs.
9. All staff work together to make the school run effectively.
10. Students would rather be in this school than transfer to another.
11. Staff would rather be at this school than transfer to another.
12. There is someone in this school upon whom I can rely.
13. The staff really cares about the students.
14. Each student's special abilities (intellectual, artistic, social, or physical) are challenged.
15. Performance expectations are tailored to the individual student.
16. Teachers use a wide range of teaching materials and media.
17. Students have opportunity for learning in individual, small group, and classroom groups.
18. The school's program encourages students to develop self-discipline and initiative.
19. Staff enforces the rules fairly.
20. The school provides reasonable alternatives to suspension.

21. Students are apprehensive about their own personal safety in the halls, restrooms and lunch area.
22. Are our students apprehensive about their own personal safety in the halls, the restrooms, and lunch area?

From Gonzales, Luis, D. (n.d.) *School Climate: 180 Degree Turn, Negative to Positive.* Los Angeles, California, Division of Evaluation, Attendance and Pupil Services, Los Angeles County Office of Education.[7]

family, or a dysfunctional family." I heard one teacher tell me that some of them are her "bused" students (meaning African American students from the other side of town). These are various ways of saying that any positive change is out of our hands: "There is nothing we can do."

A researcher by the name of Emmy Werner, along with her colleague Ruth Smith, conducted a longitudinal study in Hawaii of young people with similar backgrounds to determine why some of their lives turned out positive and why some of their lives turned out more negative. Their goal was to isolate those factors that made the difference. First described in their book, which was originally published in 1982, entitled *Vulnerable but Invincible,* many credit them with introducing the concepts of *protective factors* and *resiliency.* According to Werner, "The range of human development outcomes is determined by the balance between risk factors, stressful life events and transitions, and protective factors." She came up with the following "protective factors," which preferably occur in the home, the school, and the community.

- Caring and supportive relationships
- High expectations
- Opportunities to be involved in and contribute to their community

Protective factors are those "traits, conditions, situations, and episodes that appear to alter—or even reverse—predictions of negative outcomes and enable individuals to circumvent life stressors."[8]

Whenever I have the opportunity to speak at faculty meetings, I tell the group assembled that these three components are things that we can and do control. There are some things we have little control over, but in our schools there are practices and beliefs that are within our realm of power, and we can build them into our schools. They include:

- How we structure the school and the daily school experiences.
- The support and accommodations we provide.
- The sense of caring and positive expectations we impart to the students.
- The opportunities for participation, contributing to the school community, and for accomplishment.

These are things that are within our control, that are within our power.

"A school can create a 'coherent' environment, a climate, more potent than any single influence—teachers, class, family, neighborhood—so potent that for at least six hours a day it can override almost everything else in the lives of children."[9]

One of the key goals of a dropout prevention specialist (DPS) is to help make the school environment as welcoming, nurturing, and stimulating as is humanly possible. Some examples follow:

> The greatest effect we have on student achievement is created by establishing a school with a positive climate based on treating students with kindness and mutual respect. The mutual respect fosters an environment in which no one wants to let the other down, which results in a general sense of security felt by both students and teachers. (Union Alternative School, Tulsa, Oklahoma)[10]

> School climate refers to the character and quality of school life as experienced by students, staff and caregivers. It encompasses the norms, goals and values of a school, the interpersonal relationships, the teaching, learning and leadership practices, and the organizational structures.[11]

> A truly safe school is one in which all students feel like they belong, that they are valued, and that they are physically and emotionally safe.[12]

> A school is likely to be successful with at-risk students to the extent that the culture of the school promotes two thing; (1) academic engagement, and (2) school membership. Both of these factors are important in reducing the number of students who drop out. Engagement has emerged as an important part of the educational process and a powerful precursor to dropping out. Students who

are engaged in school, whether in the academic arena or the social arena, are more likely to attend, to learn, and eventually to finish high school; students who are disengaged are not.[13]

School membership requires the student and the school to establish a reciprocal relationship based on an exchange of commitments. The theory hypothesizes that: School membership is promoted by the following adult practices: (1) actively creating positive and respectful relations between adults and students; (2) communicating concern about students personal problems; (3) providing active help in meeting institutional standards of success and competence and (4) helping students identify a future place in society based on a link between self, school, and one's future.

In exchange for this energetic and active commitment from the institution, students are to provide their own commitment. This includes: (1) behaviors that are positive and respectful toward adults and peers; and (2) academic engagement, or a level of mental and physical effort in school tasks that makes their own achievement likely and makes the commitment of adults rewarding.[14]

The Role of the Teacher

We know that students enter our schools with many different skill levels, personal needs, a range of self-esteem and "resiliency" traits, and various levels of motivation to succeed, as well as a range of supports at home and in the community. How effectively we meet them where they are, and how we assist them in addressing and enhancing these differing levels and needs, can have a profound impact on their entire lives. Teachers are crucial in addressing the needs of their students, as well as in having a significant impact on the overall climate of the school.

It should come as no surprise that students frequently turn to and confide in a teacher whom they trust; most often this is a trust that the teacher has nurtured with his or her students. Teachers who fail to forge meaningful connections with their students are missing a great deal about the "art of teaching." How these crucial school relationships are nurtured and supported will say a great deal about how a school keeps students until graduation. Essays that contain far too many truths to be fiction, stories about thoughts of hurting oneself and secret crushes are just a few of the papers that may come to the teacher's attention. How the teacher proceeds with this information will be crucial to its outcome.

Although the DPS is usually not involved in teaching responsibilities, it is important to consider the following points for your school with regard to teaching and learning. A particularly moving statement on the role of the teacher follows:

> I have come to a frightening conclusion.
> I am the decisive element in the classroom.
> It is my personal approach that creates a climate.
> It is my daily mood that makes the weather.
> As a teacher I possess tremendous power to make a child's life miserable or joyous. I can be a tool of torture or an instrument of inspiration.
> I can humiliate or humor, hurt or heal,
> In all situations, it is my response that decides whether a crisis will be escalated or de-escalated, it is my response that decides whether a child will be humanized or de-humanized.[15]

Acknowledge that academically disconnected and at-risk students need a warm embrace to get them to school, and a challenging and interesting curriculum to keep them there.[16]

Teachers can instill a sense of "hope" for a positive future. Here are some of the ways that teachers reinforce positive mental health in children. These may be particularly relevant for elementary age children, but can have an effect on children and youth or all ages. Teachers:

- Listen with an open and clarifying ear—they question uncritically and at times in a way that elicits mastery and problem solving.
- Try to clarify what the student is trying to express
- Are accessible
- Are neutral—and don't take sides (or try not to!)
- Are accepting
- Respect confidentiality
- Are empathetic
- Help to identify and differentiate feelings, and help the student to put them into words
- Model unshakable integrity
- Set limits—teachers let the children know they are concerned with the safety of all and care enough to set limits.
- Invite curiosity—and involve the child in planning with them
- Reinforce

- Support
- Encourage mastery—the full potential within each individual child
- Provide warmth and caring—behind every correction.[17]

School Climate/Culture as a Therapeutic Intervention

I strongly believe that the school itself can be and is a therapeutic tool for children and youth. Often, mental health workers either based or linked to the school provide individual or group clinical services to a student(s) 1 or 2 hours a week. The effects of these interventions can be reinforced or have a counter-therapeutic effect in the environment of the school, its climate, and its culture.

It is nothing less than the totality of experiences that a student has each day, each week, and each month that supports the positive "therapeutic effect" and helps to build a positive sense of self. These daily experiences can and do have an effect on how well a given student will be successful in school and whether they will "hang in there" until graduation. When a student is fully engaged in the school community, he or she has created a "bond" to the school, and this should be the goal for each and every student.

Our hope is for the school to be a "caring community" with many positive relationships, high expectations, and opportunities for young people to be involved in their community and to make a contribution. To the extent that the climate and culture of the school is one that provides the necessary structures and support and joins with the other resources of the community, including educators, mental health practitioners, and community-based services and programs, the "therapeutic" potential of the school for both individual students of concern and for all students will be significant. It will, of course, have a significant effect on preventing students from dropping out.

We know that students who find strong social and emotional support are much more likely to be successful academically and to stay in school until graduation. There is a important link between the climate and culture of the school and the student's motivation to learn. Yet some 20% of elementary school students feel physically or emotionally unsafe, often feeling that there is no adult they can turn to for support. It is estimated that only 6–13% of children and youth are getting the mental health assistance they need. *For many students, the help and support they need will either be provided at school, through the school, or not at all.* Sometimes this means individual therapy in the school setting, sometimes it means the corrective experiences they have in the milieu (climate/culture) of the institution, sometimes it is a combination of the two, and, regretfully, sometimes it is neither.

I have always believed that the purpose of mental health and education to be essentially the same, that being *to nurture the positive developmental thrust of childhood and adolescence and help to overcome any stumbling blocks to its progression.*

By providing as many if the components of the resiliency research in the environment of our schools, we will be supporting positive growth and development and going a long way to preventing students from dropping out.

I remember an 8th-grade girl in one of the middle schools where I served. She was a large girl, quite mature for her age; she appeared to have poor self-esteem and was somewhat alienated by her peers. We tried to offer her some professional mental health counseling but she would have no part in seeing a "shrink." One of the student-centered components we had recently developed was a student store where students could use points they had earned or cash to purchase "swag" that interested them. We decided that it would be good to have a manager for the store, and we asked this girl if she was willing to take on the job. She said she would and jumped right into the role with vigor. She did an outstanding job, her mood and attitude improved, and I believe her overall self-esteem grew tremendously as she took on this leadership role. In this instance, we utilized the environment of the school, with the many opportunities that were created for students to become involved, to be the "treatment of choice" if you will, one that she could accept, and one that helped. It was the "milieu" of the school that helped to achieve the therapeutic effect in this instance. It was the pro-therapeutic culture of the school, the nurturing environment that had been created, that was able to stimulate the involvement of this and many other students, and, yes, that helped them to stay in school.

In addition to the students, the adult environment of the school should reflect an atmosphere of colleagues working together, with many forms of teamwork and good morale. When these things are present, they not only benefit the adults, but the feeling or tone of the school transfers over to the students—another "therapeutic benefit" to them.

How we create the climate of our school; how we develop the range of academic and supportive programs within the school; and the extent to which we provide caring and supportive relationships, high expectations, and opportunities for students to be meaningfully involved and to contribute their energies and ideas—these are the things we have some control over: these are things we can do something about.

Questions to think about:

1. How do you view the climate of your school? Is it positive or negative?
2. If you had a child of the age that your school serves, would you send him or her there?
3. What can you, as the DPS, do to improve the climate and culture of the school?

6

Handling Misbehavior
Building Positive Relationships

Current disciplinary practices in US public schools are largely based on punishing and removing students from school. Moreover, corporeal punishment is legal in 21 states, and is used frequently in 13 states. Rather than resulting in more productive behaviors, studies have shown that students who are physically punished are more likely to engage in aggressive and violent behavior toward their siblings, parents, teachers and peers in school.

There is a need to move to a new model of school discipline that is proactive, preventive, and relationship based, and that focuses on connecting students with schools rather than punishing and excluding them. It is important to note that suspension is often perceived by students as an officially sanctioned school holiday, and may be perceived as a reward rather than punishment. This would appear to be especially true for students who have nothing to lose by being suspended because they were already failing in school. In addition, suspensions have been shown to be a moderate to strong predictor of dropping out of school, and dropping out in turn triples the likelihood that a person will be incarcerated later in life. One study found that students who have been suspended are three times more likely to drop out by the 10th grade than students who have never been suspended.[1]

Promising new shifts have occurred as school districts begin moving away from exclusionary practices toward those focused on building relationships and treating

The Dropout Prevention Specialist Workbook. Howard M. Blonsky, Oxford University Press (2020). © Oxford University Press. DOI: 10.1093/oso/9780190090845.003.0008

discipline as an opportunity to support student's healthy social-emotional development. This movement is aligned with research indicating that supportive and genuine relationships are essential in creating a positive school climate, reducing problem behaviors, and lessening racial discipline gaps. Students' perceptions of positive relationships at school are predictors of a variety of behavior outcomes, such as fighting, substance use, skipping school, and academic success as measured by student grades and credits earned.

Conversely, the absence of strong positive relationships is a predictor of negative psychological outcomes like depression, suicide attempts, low self-esteem, along with adverse academic outcomes such as grade retention. Building positive and meaningful relationships is important for all students; however, it is imperative that school staff intentionally cultivate relationships with students of color as these students often report feeling less safe, and less connected to, adults in the school.[2]

A Few Thoughts

- Being acknowledged by someone, welcomed into the world each morning, is as important to a child as a good breakfast. Acknowledgment "breaks the fast" of a lonely night, providing essential nutrients for the spirit.
- The most powerful rewards are the unexpected ones because they reward a child not for what he has done, but simply for who he is.
- Give a discouraged student one task that makes him feel important. One clear reason for him to walk in the door.
- The hurt that troubled children create is never greater than the hurt they feel.
- On occasion I hear from teachers or parents, "I don't like you when. . . ." Could anyone possibly mean that? Criticize the behavior, never the child. "I don't like what you are doing" leaves the child intact.
- Try to find something positive in every child. No matter what negative behavior she or he has done, everyone has positive aspects of themselves that can be recognized.

Another consistently noted approach for relationship building is to use the beginning of the school day as an opportunity to check in with students to find out what is going on in their lives. This can set a positive tone for the rest of the day. Specific practices included personal greetings as students enter the building or classroom, advisory periods that integrate social-emotional learning activities, and regularly held classroom-based, grade-level, or school-wide morning meetings.

Most students believe, support, and expect rules of behavior; however, it is important to them that whatever rules exist are fairly, consistently, and equitably enforced. They want to feel safe in their schools, and they do not want a disorderly campus. The students are very perceptive and are the best advisors of what is fairly, consistently, and equitably enforced. The word gets around fast.

Many schools make the mistake of only responding to a particular behavior or set of behaviors rather than trying to understand what the student is telling us by his or her behavior. Either directly or indirectly students draw attention to themselves in ways that often mask the actual reason they are exhibiting a given behavior, such as:

- "Look at me/talk to me/Be with me
- I'm unhappy
- I'm mad
- I'm sad
- I'm frustrated
- I'm tired
- I need something
- I want something
- Or maybe even, I'm hungry

Some of the things the student may actually need and want are:

- Attention
- Reinforcement
- Rules that are clear, purposeful, consistent, and caringly enforced
- Logical consequences for misbehavior
- Acknowledgment
- A feeling of mastery
- Limits

The Dropout Prevention Specialist Workbook

- Modeling
- A reward
- Feedback from those who are affected by the behavior
- A feeling of comfort
- Opportunities for growth and the accompanying increase of responsibility
- Relaxation
- Food
- Unconditional love[3]

Try to promote an atmosphere that is pro-active, not reactive.

7

100% Attendance
Myth or Reality?

An effective attendance program must be at the forefront of any school's program if it is to survive as a school. The mark of an effective attendance program can be measured by the school's ability and effectiveness in bonding students to the school institution and, within it, the staff and academic, extracurricular, and social programs it offers.

This sounds somewhat simple, but this task is extremely complex and multifaceted, calling first for an understanding of the issues and then the development and/or alignment of programs and services in a wide variety of areas, both at the school and district levels. It involves issues seemingly as simple as keeping accurate classroom attendance records, to special programs that help students who have fallen by the wayside to "re-enter," extensive outreach to parents and the community, structures in place for addressing attendance issues, and a continuum of supports, both academic and social, for the students and, by extension, their families.

I want to make a few points that seem very obvious but often are not considered or implemented fully in a school.

1. Each school must reinforce the need for teachers to keep full and accurate attendance records for every student.
2. Parents must be notified after each unexcused absence, whether full- or partial-day. I recall being continually amazed by the number of parents who claimed they were never informed about their youngsters' truancy issue until the problem was completely out of control. This responsibility can be completed by teachers, an attendance clerk, a parent liaison, a counselor, or a combination of these individuals. If a school decides to use an "auto-caller," it should be set for a time when parents/caregivers

The Dropout Prevention Specialist Workbook. Howard M. Blonsky, Oxford University Press (2020).
© Oxford University Press.
DOI: 10.1093/oso/9780190090845.003.0008

are apt to be home, such as early in the morning or around the dinner hour.

3. Each school should establish a school attendance review team (SART). Refer to Chapter 3 for a description of a SART and staffing. The efforts of the SART should start with creating positive attendance practices that can have the effect of recognizing and honoring good attendance.

4. Parents must be provided written notifications of truancy. A first declaration of truancy can be sent after three unexcused absences, a second declaration after four unexcused absences, and a third declaration after five unexcused absences. Upon sending a second notification of truancy, parents should be invited to meet with a member or members of the SART, and a written contract should be one of the outcomes of that meeting.

Key Considerations for an Effective Attendance Program

Box 7.1 is an attendance assessment tool taken from a publication of the Los Angeles County Office of Education.[1] The importance of this tool being part of a manual on school climate cannot be emphasized enough.

This brief questionnaire works to identify and point out some of the multitude of factors that may be contributing to an effective attendance program—or lack of same—at the school. This should be done before planning any action to address the challenges of righting the issues identified throughout the questionnaire.

Let's take a closer look at some of the contributing factors of dropping out, listed in Chapter 1, in the section "Possible Predictors/Factors in Students Dropping Out." The groupings are as follows:

- Personal factors of the student
- Student factors related to school
- Family factors
- School structures/system factors
- Community related factors
- Vision/leadership barriers

Personal Factors of the Student

More often than not, truancy is the tip of the iceberg, a sign that something is wrong. On the one hand, our job is to carry out our legal responsibilities with regard to truancy; on the other hand, our other responsibility is to try to

---

Box 7.1 Attendance Assessment Tool

Yes: _____No:_____

1. Does our school have an effective attendance policy?
2. Is our attendance policy clear to everyone?
3. Is our law enforcement agency a member of our "attendance team?
4. Does our school have a wide variety of extracurricular activities?
5. Is good attendance positively reinforced among students?
6. Is good attendance positively reinforced among the staff?
7. Are students involved in the decisions that affect them?
8. Does a local school attendance review board (SARB) exist in our community?
9. Does a potential dropout identification and prevention program exist?
10. Is our attendance communicated regularly to staff, students, and parents?
11. Does our school have an effective counseling program with an attendance component?
12. Do opportunities exist for the nontraditional pursuit of a high school diploma?
13. Are social skills and personal responsibility offered as part of the school's curriculum?
14. Is there consistent enforcement of all policies for staff and students?
15. Does a school newspaper exist that publicizes the school's activities as well as attendance and disciplinary practices?
16. Do our staff members have opportunities for in-service activities that address issues such as teaching styles, cultural awareness, classroom management, and community relations skills?

understand what is underlying this behavior and to assist in any way possible to address what this behavior is telling us.

Referring back to the resiliency research, we know that *caring and supportive relationships* in the school can make a significant impact on socially isolated or other youngsters who feel alienated from school. *Mentoring programs* can be very effective in nurturing the personal bonds of connection between adults and youth. There is an old saying in education, "we have to reach them before we can teach them." Many schools put together a list of "at-risk" students and provide an opportunity for staff to select one or more students who they agree to mentor. The mentoring relationship includes regularly checking attendance and other indicators and keeping in close contact with the student and his or her family. Linking low-achieving high school juniors and seniors with volunteer business people is a similar mentoring strategy. Mentors can have lunch with the student at school or in the community on occasion, give their mentee a birthday or holiday card or small gift. The mentor can also serve as an advocate around issues with teachers or other staff or simply provide a friendly ear, efforts which can all be very helpful. Many schools find ways to provide a small stipend for those who serve as mentors to help defray the cost of any meals, movies, and gifts that may be provided. Many schools also provide a breakfast or luncheon for all of the students being mentored, along with their mentors. Note that it is important that parental permission be obtained before mentors venture out into the community with a student as in this day and age contacts such as this can be easily misinterpreted. A modification of the mentoring approach is to identify adults in the school who have the best relationship with individual students and give them the responsibility to phone these students when they are absent and give them a personal message on how important the student is to the smooth functioning of the school and how much that person would like to see the student in school. These identified adults could also send positive notes home.

One school in Alabama set aside 10 minutes at the end of the day during which everyone in the school would write on an index card one successful experience they had during the school day. In this program, called One Positive Experience, students found that if they had a successful experience two or three days in a row, there was a good possibility that the next day would also hold a positive happening for them. The hypothesis becomes self-fulfilling.

Support groups, or discussion groups, are another way for students to feel connected and to have their worries and concerns listened to by caring adults. Whether professional support staff is available at school or not, help can often be obtained through the school by the relationships the school has established with local public or community agencies and their representatives. School staff who are willing and able to extend themselves to address the barriers that people may have in following through with special services can be very helpful. This may include phone calls or even accompanying the student and family to a first visit. As previously stated, the school can also be used as a "bridge to services" by inviting a particular agency representative in to meet with the family at school, thereby taking away some of the mystery of this faceless person or the agency the family is being referred to.

Some schools are setting up special programs within the school to provide closer monitoring of students who are starting to fall through the cracks. One such program is the Student Support and Assistance model, where those students who have truancy patterns are grouped together into a special homeroom and are checked early in the morning and before school ends in the afternoon. Other services such as regular meetings with parents, life skills discussions being integrated into the classes, and special events or outings can be included as part of the program.

When students know they are being closely monitored and that the lines of communication are open between families and other significant people in their lives, they tend to get the idea that there are far fewer "cracks" to walk through and that their behavior is being closely watched; they tend to get the message.

Those youth who are far more alienated from school, from their families, and from any adult relationship that is meaningful may require intervention through a district or county SARB, or even through the courts. Structures need to be put in place for the school to refer to these other points on the intervention continuum. The district or county may offer *alternative program schools* for these youth that are better able to serve special need populations. (See "Components of Successful Alternative Programs" in the Appendix.)

Student Factors Related to School

Many students fall behind in their work, either as a result of not mastering the basic skills in the early grades or through missing so much school that they miss many of the developmental steps in their learning. Students are very sensitive to the messages they receive, or perceive—rightly or wrongly—from the adults in school as well as from their peers. Many students feel inadequate or worse due to the reality of their poor mastery of both skills and subject matter, and they are afraid of exposure of this fact to other youth and to adults alike. Many behavioral problems serve as a cover to low self-esteem. Our schools are filled with large numbers of students who have undiagnosed learning difficulties and emotional problems; therefore, our schools need to be sensitive to the signs of what student behavior is telling us and hopefully also have a range of supportive programs and services in place to help students overcome these barriers to achievement. This is one reason that the *student success team* (SST) process, described in Chapter 3, is so important. Although the number of students with truancy problems can be very large and it may not be possible to hold an SST on every one of these students, certainly a number can benefit from such a process to better understand the root causes of their truancy. When an SST meeting is held for a student with an attendance issue, a member of the SART should also be in attendance.

Through a careful analysis of test score data, grades, and courses failed, schools can and should work to address these disparities by providing tutorial assistance, learning labs, and other supportive ways to strengthen the skills and mastery of these students. *Being responsive to the needs of students, as they are manifested in various ways, is one of the only ways to improve attendance and success for the greatest majority of students.*

As students get older, many start to fall behind in credits. This problem is compounded when the school schedule doesn't allow sufficient opportunities to make up failed courses (i.e., credit recovery options). A practice in some schools that often discourages students who have been absent for many days is to inform them that they have already failed a course due to poor attendance. While it is certainly within a teacher's right to fail a student who has missed 20% of the semester, it is often a better message to a returning student to tell them that they can still make up partial credit or *variable credit*. This allows the student to still salvage some credit for the course, say two or three credits (based on a five-credit per course system) rather than failing all five. If they later transfer to a continuation high school or remain in a school where some independent work can be completed to make up the missed credits, the entire course does not have to be lost and later repeated, especially when the school schedule would make that very difficult.

One particular growing population comprises immigrant students who come to this country without having had the years of formal education that many of their American counterparts have had. They are often placed in a grade relative to their age even though they are quite behind in their years of schooling. *It is important for schools, particularly those that serve a large number of newcomers, to have a range of programs and services, including newcomer assistance, culturally identified clubs, and pre-literate courses, along with a continuum of English-language instruction courses based on need.* Regretfully, too many of our non-native speakers new to our schools never seem to get a foothold in their new school culture; they quickly start to miss school and, before long, they drop out.

As a dropout prevention specialist (DPS) you are always "joining" with teachers and other school staff. You are all part of the fabric of support in the school, and, by working together, the entire climate and the culture will benefit and fewer students will drop out.

Improving Teaching and Learning: Relationships, Rigor, and Relevance

> *If a child has not learned to read by the end of 1st grade, they only have a 1 in 8 chance of graduating from high school, except with a great deal of extra help. By the end of 3rd grade, the die is cast.[2]*

Some additional suggestions to improve teaching and learning include

1. Promote active learning that embraces teaching and learning strategies that engage and involve students in the learning process.
2. Expect more "Socratic" and hands-on teaching and learning experiences.
3. Develop materials to support the diverse learning strategies of our students in a manner that benefits all students.
4. Provide small-group instruction to students to address the weaknesses identified on the subtest scores of state assessments.
5. Coordinate intra- and interdepartmental instructional objectives, sequence, and course competencies, as well as integrated courses and study guides.
6. Move toward courses that are identified by competency objectives as well as course content.
7. Develop common marking codes for all essay work so that students have a better understanding of teacher corrections.

Family Factors

The research is clear that parents who have not graduated from high school, who have low incomes, are absent from the home, or are uninvolved with their youngsters present stressors for the student that are difficult to overcome and often contribute to poor attendance and dropping out. At the same time, no matter what their position is on the social scale of life, parents want the best for their children, and they hope that their youngsters will have better lives than they may have had themselves. This is the part of the parent that we must work to engage, using whatever strengths and positives that are there to join with them as a partner with the school on behalf of their youngster. It often takes a great deal of outreach to engage parents/caregivers who may be dealing with many stressors in their own life, but the rewards of engaging them can be great. As we get to know these families, we find that they may need assistance with medical issues, housing, continued educational opportunities, family counseling, legal assistance, etc. The school representative, such as the DPS, as an extension of the school's responsibility to the child, can help with community connections that will help to strengthen the entire family unit.

Many times there are individuals in the school who can establish a relationship with the family either because there is a common cultural or language connection or an already established relationship, or simply a willingness to reach out. It may require a great deal of flexibility to find time to connect with these families by phone or in person. In any case, *we want to instill the message that in order for their youngster to have increased success in school, we need them as much as they need us. We want to become partners with them for the benefit of their student.*

Many times the parent is not sure what she or he can do, and the school can provide ideas to them that are clearly within their power to implement, such as keeping in close communication with the school counselor, daily or weekly attendance checks, some sort of reward (this does not need to be monetary) when good news comes home, following through with a community referral, setting a special time and place for homework, helping to organize the youngster's backpack, making sure the student gets the tutoring, etc. In a sense, *we are working to empower* the parent to those things that are, or can be, clearly within their control.

In order to be successful in reducing the number of dropouts we need to "join" with the parents/caregivers on behalf of their youngster. Here are a few ideas to make these connections more effective:

1. Help caregivers to feel welcome and respected by the school staff, no matter their level of education or cultural background.
2. Expand "parent" resource centers within schools where parents can obtain information and develop skills for reinforcing student learning and behavior at home.
3. Develop a **Better Reading Through Parents** program that provide classes for parents to help them to develop skills that can be used to increase their child's reading ability.
4. **Parent Empowerment Groups** can help parents to work more effectively with their children, and to motivate them toward educational achievement.
5. In partnership with community colleges and adult education programs, offer **English as a Second Language** classes at the school to adult newcomers.

Questions to Think About:

1. What are the ways the DPS can increase active substantial participation of parents/guardians with the school?
2. What advantages does active parent involvement bring to the school?
3. What can you do, as the DPS, to increase family involvement at your school?

Useful readings:

1. Lawson, Hal, et al., From Parent Involvement to Parent Empowerment and Family Support: A Resource Guide for School Community Leaders, Oxford, OH: Institute for Educational Renewal, Miami University, 1998
2. Debunking the Myth About Minority Parents, Educational Horizons, Summer, 1989

School Structure/System Factors

System renewal calls for a continuing process of evaluating goals and objectives related to school policies, practices, and organizational structures as they impact a diverse group of learners.[3]

How often does school staff blame the "victim" without looking at our own house to see if we may be contributing to the problem? Are there things we can learn from what our outcomes and experiences are telling us? The State of Iowa undertook a study of whether the polices, practices, and procedures were contributing to the dropout problem in that State. Would you believe that they came up with 121 recommendations?[4]

What follows is a listing of suggested action strategies that came out of the Stay in School Coalition in San Francisco Unified over a two year period. They include items under such headings as **Infrastructure, Curriculum and Instruction, Interagency and Community Coordination, Parent Involvement, Guidance and Counseling, and the Enforcement of Truancy laws.** These are things that the Coalition believes could be done better. Hopefully these suggestions may benefit those of you in other schools and districts.

1. Fully utilize school district software to compile accurate truancy data, produce daily reports and track truant students, including an accurate profile of chronically absent students.
2. Generate a list of tips for school personnel on taking attendance and communicating with the home.
3. Multiple levels of reading and math assistance should be offered at every school.
4. Develop multiple and varied pathways to earn a recognized certificate/diploma.
5. Expand the possibilities for increased differential instruction in the classroom.
6. Re-emphasize the teaching of the crucial skills for success in high school. (See 21 crucial skills for success in Chapter VIII on the 9th grade experience.)

7. Increase intra and interdepartmental coordination and articulation of instructional sequence, grading and assignment correction practices, in order to better address standards.

8. Re-entry classes should be created at all large high schools. (See Components of Successful Alternative Programs in the Appendix.)

9. Increase the GED pathway at alternative schools.

10. Program students for English and Social Studies with the same teachers for groups of students so that reading lists and writing assignments can be complimentary.

11. Consider a school within a school structure where students and teachers are grouped into "learning pods" or "small learning communities."

12. Create a comprehensive orientation program for all incoming 9th grade students.

13. Develop additional vocational options for both general and special education students.

14. Expand "pre-literate" instructional offerings for newcomer students.

15. Allow students to waive lower level course requirements by taking a test or passing a higher level course.

16. Increase partnerships with community colleges for dual enrollment and **Step to College** programs.

17. Create a universal intake form that agencies and institutions can use for intake and gaining parental permission, giving them access to student information, and making relevant information available to each other.

18. Develop a list of contact people at each city agency and community-based organization who are specifically designated to handle truancy issues.

19. Create advocacy tools for parents to help answer such questions as "What can I do" to keep my student on track.

20. Form parent support groups facilitated by counselors to assist parents to take an active role in the child's academic progress.

21. Expand "summer bridge" programs that can ease the transition from 8th grade to the 9th grade. (The transition from middle to high school is when we lose the greatest majority of students.)

22. Create a functioning School Attendance Review Team (SART) at every school that contains three elements: **prevention, early intervention and intensive intervention**. Each element calls for different strategies that need to be considered and developed.

Many school districts have adopted policies that all students will undertake a college preparatory curriculum that prepares them for higher education, but many feel that these more rigorous requirements put many students at-risk who may not be college bound. In the report, Ready or Not: Creating a High School Diploma that Counts, it is "suggested that states should support and encourage different approaches, or "multiple pathways," to help students meet the standards, including vocational programs, project-based learning, charter schools, and advanced coursework."[5] There is no single approach that works for all students, and having a variety of alternatives may help to serve diverse interests and needs.

Community-Related Factors

The fact that youth development opportunities in the community may be few, that violence plagues many of our neighborhoods, that safety on the buses is often problematic, that jobs for youth are often few and far between, that the drug culture is prevalent, and that many of our youths have been exposed to trauma, cannot be ignored. This is the reality for many in the inner city, and increasingly for all population areas. So, this begs the question, "what can we do, if anything? We know from the resiliency research, as I have already made reference to, **Caring and Supportive Relationships, High Expectations and Opportunities to be involved in meaningful ways and to participate** should occur in the home, the school and the community. The best we can do is to try to nurture and connect with those aspects of the community that are working to provide these necessary components, and work to engage our youth in what positive programs and services that are offered in the community. Therefore, it is very important for school personnel (especially the DPS) to be knowledgeable about the range of offerings in the community, and to develop connections with them. The personal relationships the DPS has with key individuals in these agencies and programs can serve as a "bridge" for our students to make those positive connections. A couple of examples are as follows:

1. **The Twelve-Together Program**:
   This is a community-based program that organizes groups of twelve ninth graders in each of twenty Detroit high schools into weekly peer counseling sessions. Six poorly achieving students and six successful students are selected for each peer group. With the assistance of adult volunteers, the students learn to express their personal and educational

issues/problems, and to find support through the group. Program components include a student pledge to participate and to study at least one and a half hours a night and to attend the meetings. The program is based on the theory that positive peer pressure can help teenagers deal effectively with their own problems and support one another.

2. **Recognize and Involve Cliques, Gangs and Clubs**:
   A school in Riverside County enlisted the support of a group that had a reputation of being "bad." In short, these students were able to raise money for Thanksgiving and Christmas packages for needy families in the community. They, in turn, received recognition as contributors to the school's goals. The same was done with the Chicano M.E.C.H.A., the Black Student Union (BSU), and other student organizations. With the proper approach these groups of youth can become some of the strongest positive leaders within the school community, or the most influential negative force.

3. **Adopt-A-Student**:
   This program, adopted in Atlanta, and adopted in many other communities, pairs business volunteers as mentors or "big brothers/ sisters" with low achieving high school students. Through the relationship with the volunteer and monthly job preparation workshops, students are encouraged to finish high school and to develop post high school career plans. The Atlanta public schools and the Merit Employment Association jointly run the Atlanta program.

4. **Beacon Center Programs**:
   Many schools across the Country are developing community centers within schools, (sometimes referred to as community schools).
      These centers serve both the youth and the adults in the community before and after school, on the weekends and during holiday periods. They offer a variety of social, recreational and academic support programs that serve to keep students engaged in useful/productive activities, and to obtain needed services. Most of these programs are jointly funded by the school district, private foundations or businesses, and often times, public dollars, as is the case in New York and San Francisco.

The bottom line is that the school cannot live and thrive in isolation from the community. To the extent that staff members are involved in neighborhood committees and activities, the bond between the school and the community is strengthened.

Vision/Leadership Barriers

One of the biggest barriers we face in education is those who, for whatever reason, do not believe we can do better. For some, they may have experienced many years of frustration. There may be an unwillingness to look at all of the factors that contribute to the problem, including those things that the school or system may be contributing to the problem itself. Negative beliefs often present a significant blockage for those who wish to try new and creative approaches. As previously stated in this workbook, I believe the worst of these are those who put all of the blame on the students, the parents or the communities.

I strongly believe it is important to continue to put forth ideas to those in leadership positions, through committee work, by submitting written proposals, or by direct discussion, those things that we believe may make the situation better. So, is 100% attendance a myth or can it be a reality? I believe we can do better, whether we hit the 100% marker or not. I sincerely hope that some of the ideas in this Chapter have given you some renewed hope and a few strategies. By working together, we can continue to make an important difference in the lives of our students and their families, as well as our schools.

Questions to think about:

1. Do the various factors/forces that contribute to "early school leaving" make sense as they are more fully explained?
2. Can you think of any other strategies to address the factors that have been listed? If so, what are they?
3. From the items you have found in this workbook, and other suggestions you have, can you start to visualize a comprehensive dropout prevention and recovery plan and program in our school and/or district? Please make a list of them.
4. Do you have any thoughts about what the first steps are in your school and/or district?
   What would they be?

8

The 9th-Grade Experience

Ninth grade marks a critical juncture in American schooling. Students who manage the academic demands of the transition to high school have a high probability of graduating four years later. But those who do not—who fail to earn as many credits as they should have during the 9th grade—face a significantly elevated risk of dropping out of high school.

The strongest evidence points to inadequate preparation for high school and the organization of high schools. Studies of cohort groups of Philadelphia students showed that failing math or English in the middle grades was a better predictor than standardized test scores of academic difficulty in ninth grade.

The task of helping ninth graders to succeed requires the serious efforts of educators at the pre-K through eighth grade level to prepare students for the academic requirements of ninth grade. It also requires the involvement of parents in the supervision and support of their children. But, ultimately, it is high schools that bear the most immediate responsibility for putting in place the curriculum, school organizational features, and strong teachers who will increase a ninth grader's chances of making a good transition to high school.[1]

Ninth grade is where the greatest number of high school students begin to fall off course. The 22 districts participating in the conference lost 20% or more of their students during the freshman year. Of a typical cohort of 100 such ninth graders who entered in the fall were followed in the spring of what would have been their tenth

The Dropout Prevention Specialist Workbook. Howard M. Blonsky, Oxford University Press (2020).
© Oxford University Press.
DOI: 10.1093/oso/9780190090845.003.0008

grade year, only 56 had actually been promoted on time and were attending school as 10th graders. Twenty students had already dropped out, and the remaining 34 were kept back in the ninth grade. Of the 24 students retained in the 9th grade, only half were still in schools three years later.[2]

In the Los Angeles Unified School District [LAUSD] 48% of students graduated with their class in 2005. LAUSD has seen a huge loss of students in the 9th grade—34% of freshman did not move on to the 10th grade on time.[3]

Of the 780 dropouts, 376 or nearly half, have dropped out either in the transition from the 8th grade to high school (114 of the 8th grade graduates never showed up for high school), or in the 9th grade itself. (262 of the total dropouts left in the 9th grade). This would seem to suggest that if there is one grade toward which interventions might be directed to lower the dropout rate, it would be the 9th grade (including the 8th to 9th grade transition). Anything effective done in the 9th grade would most likely reduce the dropout rate in subsequent grades. 100 students dropped out in the 10th grade. By the time those who are left in the cohort get to the 12th grade, only 27 students dropped out. (San Francisco Unified School District dropout prevention plan/report, 1990)

Clearly, we must do more to ensure a smooth transition from middle school to high school and to restructure the 9th grade experience to ensure that greater numbers of students are progressing through high school. Suggestions to strengthen the "holding power" of the schools during the initial year follow:

Buddy systems: When an "at-risk" student transfers to a new school, a "buddy system" should be implemented. The "buddy system" assigns the student to a staff or student "buddy" who is trained to assist the new student to be successful in the new environment.

Orientation programs. Comprehensive orientation program for 9th graders should be in place. With an increasing number of students who enter high school with poor study and work habits and a frequent lack of understanding the structure and expectations of this setting, many high schools are moving toward a semester-long orientation program At Chief Sealth High School in Seattle, Washington, after 4 years of implementation of this program, the results show that more students wish to continue their learning through graduation, and this is borne out in the statistics. A previous 22–29% dropout rate has come down to the 12% level. The program modules are as follows[4]:

- Rules, regulations, rights, and responsibilities
- School organization and tradition
- Study skills/time management
- Library skills and study rooms
- Self-concept/self-awareness
- Multicultural human relations/values clarification
- Electives
- Communication skills
- Job-related skills/career planning/decision making
- Drug/alcohol decision making

The 9th graders were apportioned into 11 sections with a maximum of 23 students in any one class. Groups were formed to ensure balance by gender and the integration of special education and English-language learners. The rather small classes made contact between the students and the instructor more personal. All sections were taught during the first period so that all 11 segments could be rotated during the 90-day semester, with each class spending an average of 8 days in any one unit. The instruction was carried out by a staff that included teachers, the nurse, administrators, counselors, and the librarian.

Variable credit programs. As previously stated, variable, or partial credit should be available for students who have missed many days of school. This gives the teacher the opportunity to let student know they should still continue to pursue passing their class, even though the teacher feels they have not attended enough to earn full credit. For the student, it is saying to them that they have not failed the entire course and there is still some hope.

Homeroom assignments. Students should be assigned to homerooms based on the homeroom groupings they were in at the feeder middle school. This might tend to foster friendship links already established and reduce social isolation and anonymity.

Clustering. Cluster groups of students together for certain courses (i.e., language arts/social studies, math/science. This could foster increased articulation and coordination between teachers with regard to instructional sequence, as well as individual approaches with students. For students, the friendship links can help to keep them in class, and they can assist one another with homework, projects, etc.

The Dropout Prevention Specialist Workbook

Advisory periods. Some high schools are developing or reinstating advisory periods. One model assigns students in groups of 14, led by a senior student who has enough history with the school to be able to answer questions and share experiences during the discussions.

CORE programs. CORE programs could provide additional stability and consistency to 9th graders identified "at-risk" by their feeder middle schools. This program model can also be appropriate for students recovered from having dropping out and for those students who have failed a majority of classes in their first semester. Program components are as follows:

- Five teachers and a counselor work together as a team and agree to a common preparation period for planning. Focusing on individual needs, techniques and materials are shared and coordinated by the CORE team.
- The students remain as a CORE group in one classroom throughout the day; the teachers rotate to them.
- Counselor and other support staff meet with the teachers weekly.
- Parent/caregiver conferences are held with all CORE staff weekly meetings.
- Agencies involved with the individual students are invited to meet with the CORE team for coordination and planning. High school success skills can be integrated into course content. Topics can include study skills, career readiness, critical thinking, current social issues, values clarification, conflict resolution, and peer relationships.

Mentoring. Establish mentor programs; all students identified as "at-risk" should be assigned an adult mentor. The mentoring program uses trained teachers, administrators, and other support staff to have regular interactions with and monitoring of the student.

Crucial skills training. Twenty-one crucial skills for success in high school are listed on the next page. Many students entering the 9th grade are deficient in these skills, and these deficiencies will need to be addressed if the student is to be successful in high school. As stated by many authors in the field of education, an increasingly large number of students are entering high school without these prerequisite skills.

> In high poverty, non-selective inner city high schools, fewer than one in five students enters high school having reached profi- ciency levels in the eighth grade. More that 80% of ninth graders

repeat the grade or are over-age, or are in special education, or have below seventh-grade math and reading skills.[5]

Part of the reason for this is that many districts have changed "junior high schools," traditional grade 6–9 schools, to "middle schools" that serve grades 6–8 or 5–8. Therefore, the former high school of grades 10–12 is now grades 9–12. Many believe that there needs to be some sort of structure in the 9th grade that reinforces these skills for those who may be weak in this area, and, by not doing so, we may be adding to the number of students who will fall behind quite quickly and will have difficulty making it to the next grade level. Some high schools are adding an additional period at the end of the day to reinforce these skills.

- Comprehend, calculate, and do arithmetic operations
- Comprehend text reading material
- Read quickly through various materials
- Understand broad organizational patterns
- Demonstrate understanding of content through recall, recognition and explanation
- Use textbooks effectively
- Locate information quickly and accurately
- Read charts, graphs and tables
- Identify key words and important points
- Express ideas in writing
- Write legibly
- Spell correctly
- Monitor errors
- Manipulate information
- Generate and test hypothesis
- Prioritize
- Brainstorm for ideas
- Classify and make visual representations
- Problem-solve
- Take notes from lectures
- Take notes from reading material

(In addition, vocabulary development in grades 3–8 is crucial for future success in high school.)

The Dropout Prevention Specialist Workbook

Focused intervention. The City of Detroit has focused on the 9th grade as a way to reduce its dropout rate and created a budget of $16 million to go about it. Results indicate that the dropout rate declined substantially. Of the 12,200 students who entered in the 9th grade, 11.7% dropped out compared with 18.3% in the previous year.

Their program components included small learning communities (SLCs) that provide teachers an opportunity to meet regularly and discuss students' academic and personal progress so that they can better support both their students and each other. Another strategy was to hire a cadre of case managers/mentors to develop personal connections with the 9th graders, to track their progress by checking in with the students regularly, and to work with other school staff to address the challenges and issues of the students.

Box 8.1 is a document entitled *Ninth-Grade Transition Strategies Walk Through,*[6] developed by Tabitha Foreman of the Virginia Department of Education. The questions can be answered with a yes or no with regard to your school or district.

Box 8.1

Ninth-Grade Transition Strategies Walk Through

Instruction and Student Achievement
- Do ninth-grade teachers have a common planning time?
- Do teachers use special strategies with English-language learners?
- Is literacy emphasized across the curriculum?
- Are incentives provided to students for academic performance?
- Are remediation programs in existence for students?
- Does the school host a summer bridge program for entering ninth graders that includes enrichment and/or remediation in one of the core areas?
- Is there a homework policy for ninth graders?
- Does the school have a program in place aimed at improving attendance among ninth-grade students?
- Are ninth-grade students provided instruction in the development of study skills, note taking, and time management?
- Are class sizes in the ninth-grade lower than other grades?

Physical Structure

- Are ninth-grade students housed in a separate building or a separate part of the main building?
- Is the school using a small learning community (SLC) model?
- Is the school using a "school within a school" model?
- Do ninth-grade students attend a separate in-school suspension?

Social Development

- Are upperclassmen serving as mentors to freshman?
- Are teachers serving as mentors to freshman?
- Does the school have a student advisory period led by a teacher mentor or a senior student?
- Are there student recognition programs for ninth-grade students?
- Is character education part of the programming for ninth-grade students?

Guidance and Planning

- Does each ninth-grade student have a high school graduation plan?
- Do ninth-grade students participate in career planning and exploration programs?
- Is there a counselor assigned specifically to ninth-grade students?
- Do ninth-grade students receive one-on-one academic advising?

From Foreman, Tabitha. *Ninth Grade Walk Through*. Richmond: Virginia Department of Education, n.d.

Questions to think about:

1. Does your high school have any special programs or accommodations for 9th grade students, particularly those who have been identified as "at risk" in the transition from middle to high school?
2. If you are in a high school, what sort or orientation is offered to incoming 9th graders? Do you feel what your school provides is adequate?
3. If the teachers are identifying students that do not seem to have one or more of the 21 Crucial Skills for Success in High School, is anything offered to help remediate these weak areas?
4. In reviewing the Ninth-Grade Transition Walk Through, do you see any areas that your school could improve upon? If so, what are they and what role might you play in helping to address them?

The Dropout Prevention Specialist Workbook

9

Re-Engaging Out-of-School Youth

Any sensible reform effort must embrace both dropout prevention and recovery. Before we can help to re-connect out of school young people to educationally viable options, we need to understand what caused the student to leave school initially, and consider those factors in working with the youth to find an option that won't have the same result for them.

A student may proactively disconnect (e.g., engage in truancy to pursue some preferable, desired activities). Or the disconnection may be reactive—a protective form of coping stemming from motivation to avoid and protest against situations in which the student feels unable to perform and/or is coerced to participate (e.g., instruction that is too challenging, classrooms that seriously limit options; teachers who are over-controlling). The underlying motivational differences have profound implications for success in re-engaging students.

Dialogue to Establish Personalized Re-Engagement Strategies
The focus of the dialogue is on:

- Clarifying the student's perceptions of the problem by talking openly about why the student has become disengaged.
- Exploring changes that may help the student(s) to view the teacher as supportive (rather than controlling and indifferent) and to perceive course content and other educational activities as personally valuable

The Dropout Prevention Specialist Workbook. Howard M. Blonsky, Oxford University Press (2020). © Oxford University Press.
DOI: 10.1093/oso/9780190090845.003.0008

for them and obtainable. Examples include eliminating threatening evaluative measures, reframing school learning in terms of real-life needs and experiences, and enhancing expectations of personal benefits.

- Renegotiating involvement in a school setting through the development of new and mutual agreements that will be evolved over time through conferences, including caregivers when appropriate. The intent is to affect perceptions of choice, value, and probable outcome. The focus throughout is on clarifying an awareness of valued options, enhancing expectations of positive outcomes, and engaging the student in meaningful, ongoing decision making. Involve the student in sampling what is proposed and ensuring the provision for re-evaluating and modifying decisions as perceptions shift.
- Re-establish and maintain an appropriate working relationship— ensuring that ongoing interactions are designed to create a sense of trust, open communication, and to provide personalized support and direction.[1]

With roughly one-third of our young people dropping out of school— often a higher number for young people of color—recovery and reconnection must become a top priority of public school districts. Some possible models of dropout recovery include re-entry programs in traditional public schools; specially created recovery-focused schools; alternative learning centers; community-based nonprofit schools and programs; for-profit schools; feder- ally, state-, and county- funded efforts; community colleges; adult education systems; and other social services.

Regretfully, many school districts simply remove students from their rolls when they leave prior to graduation. In my own experience, that is a sorry mistake because many of these youth can be returned to a viable educational option. I was granted a Federal Dropout Demonstration grant that reached out to some 200 students who had dropped out of school. The approach utilized by our six staff members was referred to as "case management." We literally went out and knocked on doors to locate these out-of-school youth, and, when we did locate them, most were glad that we had come. Almost every one of them had little knowledge of what options were there for them. The great majority did not want to go back to the same school that they had dropped out from, as obviously that school did not work for them. They were open to hearing about what options existed for them, including enrolling at City College if they were 18 years old or had an exemption, a GED program, or a re-entry program set up in two of the high schools we worked with. The goal of re-engaging these former students is to help find a viable educational or career preparation option. *School districts must take responsibility for all of their young people and show leadership in reaching out to disconnected youth.*

Re-Entry Models

The Great Kids Come Back Campaign actively recruits students who have dropped out to return to school and finish their degree. During the 2008–2009 school year, more than 10 fairs were held and more than 350 students attended and re-enrolled in school.

The following list describes some of the re-entry models we researched and implemented.

1. A store-front location that serves as a sort of "multiservice center," where student needs can be assessed and resources and services planned, implemented, and monitored. This model includes credit recovery options and online learning packets.
2. For students recovered from having dropped out, repeat 9th graders, and those selected from the D/F course(s) grades, and the incomplete course list, the following actions are taken:
   - Students are interviewed by the teacher(s) and a dropout prevention counselor.
   - The students are programmed for three AM classes within the re-entry program (English, world civilization, and math).
   - Variable credit is offered so that students can earn one credit at a time (based on a 5-credit model for one course), helping them to see some growth and credit(s) earned rather than passing or failing the entire course. (Another plug for variable credit!)
   - The counselor works closely with these students to monitor attendance, develop and implement support services, and monitor the delivery of these services.
   - Study skills and other high school success skills are integrated into the curriculum.
3. A re-entry program at a vocational and technical high school had the following features:

- Students attend three or four academic classes in the morning with a re-entry teacher(s) and take a vocational/technical preparation program in the afternoon.
- The class is self-contained. Students stay with the same teacher in the same room all morning.
- Study skills and other high school success skills are integrated into the curriculum.

4. The Back on Track program:
   - A one-semester "back on track" transitional program for those students who are recovered from having dropped out or whose attendance is so poor that continuing in a comprehensive high school is unworkable.
   - Such a program was established in the 1990s with six staff, a program lead school social worker, two teachers, a counselor/work experience coordinator, and a peer resource/activities coordinator.
   - This program was developed out of a need defined by the students who felt they who needed a "transitional" program to prepare them for their return to another comprehensive high school (with support), a GED program, the high school proficiency exam, adult school, Job Corps, or community college.

5. The Student Support and Assistance Program (SSAP; as implemented in Florida):
   - Students are identified in the 8th grade as a "student at risk" for the possibility of dropping out in the transition to high school or in the 9th-grade year.
   - As first-semester 9th graders, students in this program take a first hour English "block" class that is co-taught by two SSAP teachers; the last 30 minutes are enrichment.
   - The last class of the day is algebra, which is taught by an SSAP teacher.
   - Check-in is done with the students twice a day.
   - Attendance is monitored by daily phone calls, home visits, and parent/caregiver conferences.
   - Character education, psychosocial assessments, psychoeducational groups, classroom guidance are offered; student portfolios are developed; and additional social work and counseling services are provided.
   - Behavior monitoring is done through behavior contracts, positive note cards that are sent home, and phone calls to the students' home. The SSAP team handles all referrals of students to this program.

- Team members include an administrator, SSAP teachers, school social worker, and guidance counselor.
6. The Continuation School and Job Corps Partnership Program:
   - Students attend a small, necessary high school in the morning for core academics.
   - Students are transferred to a Job Corps site in the afternoon for career preparation courses that can lead to apprenticeships with various unions.
7. The Pueblo High School Project Success (New Mexico):
   - The Retrieval Transition program offers four classes during periods one through four: Life Skills, English, Math, and Free Enterprise. Credit is awarded on a quarterly basis, but students are expected to remain in the program for an entire semester.
   - Mentors are matched with "at-risk" students. Each mentor selects two to five students to work with and schedules regular meetings with their mentees.
   - An alternative instruction program serves 15 students at a time with assignments that last between 5 and 10 days in length. This model can also serve as an alternative for formal suspension. Packets, developed by the coordinator, are completed by students during their stay in the program. The packets include decision making, self-assessment, goal-setting, study skills, and a career interest inventory.:
8. Partnership Academy Programs
   - These academies are partnerships between the school district, businesses, and the community.
   - The academies are "school-within-a-school" programs that engage "at-risk" students in a specific career-focused curriculum over a 3-year period.
   - Students enjoy smaller classes and increased personal attention in a centralized setting that prepares them for postsecondary education or skilled entry-level employment.
   - Each academy focuses on a particular career interest area or vocational/technical skill, combining core curriculum with a relationship to the world of work.
   - Students are allowed to "job shadow" individuals working in businesses that are an area of interest and to engage in summer internships in real work situations.

- Research studies have shown improvements in students' attitudes toward school, focus, goal setting, and completion of assignments; improved grades; increased self-esteem; and improved attendance.

9. Montgomery County (Dayton), Ohio, established an institutional and centralized city-wide system of dropout recovery for out-of-school youth. They realized that to just return these youth to the same program/schools would not work; they realized they needed a whole new system. The Out of School Youth Task Force set up the Sinclair Fast Forward Center, a clearinghouse to recover dropouts. Additional programs included Improved Solutions for Urban Systems, the Mound Street Academies (Military Careers Academy, Health Careers Academy, IT Career Academy), the Life Skills Center, a GED program, the Miami Valley Career and Technical College-Youth Connections, and the New Choices Middle School. A "high school plus" program offered both a diploma and an industry-recognized credential in one of four career fields: construction, manufacturing, healthcare, and computer technology.[2]

Questions to think about:

1. Does your school or district reach out to those students who are considered as having dropped out with the goal of re-entering them into a viable educational program? If so, what role do you or can you play?
2. Do any of the program models described in this chapter look like something that would work in your school or district?
3. If you believe one or more of the program models would be useful to your school or district, what can you, as the DPS, do to bring them about?
4. Is it the intention of your school or district to reach out to, and re-engage, out of school youth? If so, what role can you, or do you play in this effort?

The Dropout Prevention Specialist Workbook

10

Communication, Coordination, and Collaboration
School and Community Involvement

We have all heard the saying "it takes a village to raise a child." To the extent that the school and/or district joins with and forms alliances with public and community services and resources, the potential for serving students and families in a more comprehensive way is there, and the potential to curb the tide of more dropouts is there as well.

Please note that the title of this chapter is "Communication, Coordination, and Collaboration." This represents a continuum of people and agencies working together. Communication between and among service providers can be helpful, but it is certainly not coordination of services nor is it collaboration, which is the "gold standard." True collaboration involves a good deal of flexibility with regard to finances, decision making, and a focus on a common purpose and the greater good. It involves the ability to compromise and requires mutual respect, understanding and trust.

> It is important to distinguish between relationships based on co-operation, coordination and collaboration because the degree of involvement, responsibility, authority, and shared resources are different. Cooperative relationships are informal, information sharing arrangements that exist without a commonly defined mission, structure, planning effort, or sharing of resources or authority. Coordinated relationships have a more formal structure and compatible missions. There is some planning and division of roles, communication channels are established, resources are shared, but authority remains within the individual organizations. Collaborative relationships bring previously separate organizations into a new structure with full commitment to a common mission, comprehensive planning, well-defined communication channels, resources pooled and jointly dispensed,

The Dropout Prevention Specialist Workbook. Howard M. Blonsky, Oxford University Press (2020).
© Oxford University Press.
DOI: 10.1093/oso/9780190090845.003.0008

and the authority to make decisions. The success of community collaborative depends on the belief that the greatest potential for effective and positive change come from a collaborative process.[1]

Many state and federal grants, as well as foundation awards, give extra "points" to the applicants if there is collaboration with schools. Members of the collaborative see how their self-interest relates to the larger goal, one that it may not be possible to accomplish alone.

Our strategies for ensuring student success through broad and deep collaboration among all agencies, institutions and individuals who touch the lives of children are guided by the following principles:

1. We must define the outcomes we seek for all children in positive terms and align actions to achieve those positive outcomes,
2. Educators must contribute to an effective system of supports for children and families that will ensure that all children are able to achieve these positive outcomes,
3. Educators must integrate efforts to support families and better meet the developmental needs of children and youth into efforts to restructure schools,
4. These changes must take place as part of a larger national effort to ensure equitable opportunities and outcomes for all children.

An unprecedented opportunity exists for developing a common vision of what we as a nation want for our children and for mobilizing our collective resources to realize that vision. This opportunity is enhanced by a climate of reform among the systems that serve our nation's children and families. We will continue to work closely with other organizations and individuals concerned with the well-being of children and families to promote more strategic and systemic approaches to improving outcomes for all Americans. We are committed to bold, collaborative action to fulfill the promise of the principles and strategies offered and thereby guarantee the futures of all of our nation's young people.[2]

The Dropout Prevention Specialist Workbook

In recent years there has been a lot of emphasis placed on school-linked and school-based services. *School-based service* represents a service entity that is actually based at the school and integrated into the school team, with proper considerations for issues of information sharing and confidentiality. *School-linked services* represent those agencies and service providers who have a defined relationship with the school, often defined through a memorandum of understanding (MOU), but are not physically based at the school. The benefit of such a relationship may be the ability for the clients referred from the base of the school to avoid some of the "red tape" and other barriers that may deter students and families from getting services. There may be a dedicated person in the agency who has a close connection with school staff, and, by working together, they can often create a "bridge" to needed services and resources.

Best Practices

Some years ago I was involved in a project where we sought to identify the best practices and competencies for integrated and collaborative services.[3] The list of best practices includes strategic planning, systems thinking, a team approach, acknowledgment of accomplishments, governance, a behavioral/mental health perspective, evaluation, staff development, funding, an interdisciplinary approach, inclusive multicultural systems, organizational readiness, case management services, a prevention-oriented outlook, a family- and child-centered approach, an outcomes-oriented stance, a strengths-based focus, a holistic approach, accessible design, responsive/flexible operations, an advocacy-oriented approach, integrated practice, coverage with approach.

Invaluable skills, knowledge, values, attitudes, and orientation for collaborative practice include skills in team work, skills in case management, cultural competence, problem-solving skills, assessment skills, evaluation skills, group process skills, knowledge of service integration, knowledge of funding and funding sources, knowledge of governance, a strength-based orientation, an outcomes orientation, a systems level perspective, a family/consumer-oriented approach, communication skills, change agent skills, advocacy skills, leadership kills, and skills in collaboration.

This is certainly a long list of traits, beliefs, and orientations. In my experience, the most important qualities for integrated and collaborative services is something I call a *collaborative personality*. We have all been on committees where it is obvious that one or two (hopefully no more) of the members do not have this quality. They may interrupt, distract the other members from focusing on the goal, vote against the will of the larger group, and make others uncomfortable in their presence. These are members who don't just respectfully disagree with a certain vote or direction of the collaborative work; they are downright ornery and can create a coolness over the work of the group. It would be good if someone would take them aside and suggest they use their energies in another way. If, however, you are open to the perspectives and ideas of others, are willing to compromise, you believe that the whole is greater than each of its parts, have a strong commitment to teamwork, are a consensus builder, and if your focus is kept on the students and families you are working to serve—then most likely you have a collaborative personality.

Questions to think about:

1. How can you, as the dropout prevention specialist (DPS) at your school site, move the school to identify and meet the needs of at-risk students through coordinated and integrated efforts?
2. How can your school go about mapping the student support resources at your school or in your district in order to discover gaps in the current student services safety net and to eliminate any overlap?
3. What are your thoughts on how to access the significant resources available from other funding sources that include the state/federal government, community agencies, and charitable foundations?
4. What process does your school have to help students and families without duplicating services?
5. What support does the principal need to provide to make sure that all parties to the collaboration and integration of services meet on a regular basis?

Further Reading

Lawson, Hal, and Katherine Hooper-Briar. *Serving Children, Youth and Families Through Inter-professional Collaboration and Service Integration: A Framework for Action.* Orford, OH: Danforth Foundation and the Institute for Educational Renewal, Miami University,

1994. (This can be read online at Eric ED 425234 or through the UCLA Center for School Mental Health.)

Lawson, Hal, and Katherine Briar-Lawson. *Connecting the Dots: Progress toward the Integration of School Reform, School-linked Services, Parent Involvement and Community Schools.* Orford, OH: Institute for Educational Renewal, Miami University, 1997.

11

Assessing Learning Levels and Help for Students

School improvement begins and ends with assessment. However, assessment is only effective and useful if there is a plan with measurable goals and expected outcomes. The assessment of student performance and school climate can be the energizing event that moves the school to create a more effective learning environment for students. If students do not have some feeling of academic success, or even adequacy, there is a much greater chance they will drop out. The question is what does your school or district do to assess the learning levels of its students so that program modifications can be made and/or additional help can be provided? What prevention and intervention strategies can be implemented to improve attendance and academic levels?

As previously discussed, this includes what is called a *cycle of inquiry* leading to a data-driven improvement process.

The role of the dropout prevention specialist (DPS) includes participating in program assessment and accountability activities, working as a member of a team to collect and interpret data, and then creating and monitoring improvement strategies for attendance, behavior, and academics.

Questions to think about:

1. Does your school collect data about student attendance, student behavior, and student achievement? What does the school or district do with these data once they are collected?
2. Has the school formally committed itself to an improvement path in the areas of student attendance, attitude, and achievement? Are there quantitative improvement goals in all these areas? What can the DPS do to assist and encourage the school to support a formal improvement process?

The Dropout Prevention Specialist Workbook. Howard M. Blonsky, Oxford University Press (2020). © Oxford University Press. DOI: 10.1093/oso/9780190090845.003.0008

3. What kinds of data need to be collected and why?
4. Why can "disaggregating" the data be so useful?
5. Why is it necessary to use multiple measures in evaluation?
6. How can your school use attendance data to modify schedules and build programs and services?
7. Who else at the school site can be recruited to assist in proposing and supporting an improvement effort in the areas of attendance, attitude, and achievement?

Further Reading

Lawrence-Brown, Diana. Differentiated instruction: inclusive strategies for standards-based learning to benefit the whole class. *American Secondary Education* 32(3/Summer 2004), pp. 34-62. (Available online; published by Dwight Schar College of Education, Ashland University.)

Bernhardt, V. L. *Data Analysis for Comprehensive School-wide Improvement*, 3rd edition. Abingdon, UK: Routhledge Press, 2013, chapters 1–4.

Smokler, M. *Results, The Key to Continuous School Improvement*, 2nd edition. Alexandria, Virginia: ASCD, 1999.

12

Building Comprehensive Dropout Prevention and Recovery/Re-Entry Programs

Of interest is that, under the new federal education law, the Every Student Succeeds Act (ESSA), there will be increased attention paid to attendance issues. Under the new act, states will be required to report chronic absenteeism rates for schools, and school districts will be allowed to spend federal dollars on training to reduce absenteeism. The federal government has created a toolkit, entitled *Every Student, Every Day*[1] that offers information, suggested action steps, and lists of existing tools and resources, including evidence-based resources. The Toolkit is available at http://www2.ed.gov/about/inits/ed/chronicabsenteeism/toolkit.pdf. This should be a useful tool for dropout prevention specialist (DPS) workers to use to expand their knowledge and determine which ideas and approaches might be utilized at a particular school and/or district.

> Educational organizations are like jigsaw puzzles, composed of interrelated, interconnected pieces. Changing just one element may well distort the entire puzzle. Those who seek a single cure for the complex ills of education—who believe that eliminating one problem will supply the needed remedy—are destined for disillusionment. By contrast, system renewal focuses on discovering root causes, directing efforts to remove them and preventing their recurrence.[2]

Effective Strategies for Dropout Prevention

The National Dropout Prevention Center/Network has listed 15 effective strategies for dropout prevention,[3] which are presented here for your review and consideration.

The Dropout Prevention Specialist Workbook. Howard M. Blonsky, Oxford University Press (2020).
© Oxford University Press.
DOI: 10.1093/oso/9780190090845.003.0008

- *Systemic renewal*: Systemic renewal calls for a continuing process of evaluating goals and objectives related to school policies, practices, and organizational structures as they impact a diverse group of learners.
- *School–community collaboration*: When all groups in a community provide collective support to the school, a strong infrastructure sustains a caring environment where youth can thrive and achieve.
- *Safe learning environments*: A comprehensive violence prevention plan, including conflict resolution, must deal with potential violence as well as crisis management. A safe learning environment provides daily experiences, at all grade levels, to enhance positive social attitudes and effective interpersonal skills in all students.
- *Family engagement*: Research consistently finds that family engagement has a direct, positive effect on children's achievement and is one of the most accurate predictors of a student's success in school.
- *Early childhood education*: Birth-to-five interventions demonstrate that providing a child additional enrichment can enhance brain development. The most effective way to reduce the number of children who will ultimately drop out is to provide the best possible classroom instruction from the beginning of their school experience through the primary grades.
- *Early literacy development*: Early interventions help low-achieving students improve their reading and writing skills, thereby building the necessary foundation for effective learning in all subjects.
- *Mentoring/tutoring*: Mentoring is a one-to-one caring, supportive relationship between a mentor and a mentee that is based on trust. Tutoring is also a one-to-one activity that focuses on academics and is an effective practice when addressing specific needs such as reading, writing, or math competencies.
- *Service learning*: Service learning connects meaningful community service experiences with academic learning. This teaching/learning method promotes personal and social growth, career development, and civic responsibility and can be a powerful vehicle for effective school reform at all grade levels.

- *Alternative schooling*: Alternative schooling provides potential dropouts a variety of options that can lead to graduation, with programs paying special attention to the student's individual social needs and academic requirements for a high school diploma.
- *After-school opportunities*: Many schools provide after-school and summer enhancement programs that eliminate information loss and inspire interest in a variety of areas. Such experiences are especially important for students at risk of school failure because they fill the afternoon "gap time" with constructive and engaging activities.
- *Professional development*: Teachers who work with youth at high risk of academic failure need to feel supported and that they have an avenue by which they can continue to develop skills, techniques, and learn about innovative strategies.
- *Active learning*: Active learning embraces teaching and learning strategies that engage and involve students in the learning process. Students find new and creative ways to solve problems, achieve success, and become lifelong learners when educators show them that there are different ways to learn.
- *Educational technology*: Technology offers some of the best opportunities for delivering instruction to engage students in authentic learning, addressing multiple intelligences and adapting to students' learning styles.
- *Individualized instruction*: An individualized instructional program for each student allows for flexibility in teaching methods and motivational strategies that consider these individual differences.
- *Career and technical education*: A quality career vocational technical education (CVTE) program along with a related guidance program are essential for all students. School-to-work programs recognize that youth need specific skills to prepare them to measure up to the increased demands of today's workplace.

In his book, *Dropping Out: Why Students Drop Out of High School and What Can Be Done About It*,[4] Russell W. Rumberger lists three approaches (targeted, comprehensive, and systemic) to address the dropout problem. These approaches are summarized in Box 12.1.

Although countless programs and strategies have been developed
to improve dropout and graduation rates, they can be grouped into
three basic approaches: targeted, comprehensive, and systemic. The
three approaches differ in both scope and focus, and they each have
advantages and disadvantages.

Targeted Approaches

The most common approach for improving dropout and graduation
rates is to *develop a special program targeting students most at risk for
dropping out of school.* There are two targeted approaches. One is to
provide supplemental services to students within an existing school
program. The second is to provide an alternative school program,
either within an existing school (school-within-a-school model), or
in a separate facility (alternative school). Neither approach attempts
to change existing institutions serving most students; instead, the
approaches create supplemental or alternative programs that target
students who are somehow identified as being at-risk of dropping out
or who have already dropped out.

Comprehensive Approaches

The second and most common approach to dropout prevention is
through comprehensive or school-wide reform. This approach is
premised on the belief that targeted programs are insufficient to improve
dropout or graduation rates either because they are not comprehensive
enough or because they do not help enough students. Within the comprehensive umbrella, there are three approaches to dropout prevention.

A second approach to dropout prevention is through comprehensive or
school wide reform. This approach is premised on the belief that targeted
programs are insufficient to improve dropout or graduation rates either
because they are not comprehensive enough or because they do not help
enough students. There are three comprehensive approaches to dropout
prevention. One is to reform existing high schools. Comprehensive
School Reform (CSR) involves multiple strategies to alter all facets of a

school and is built on the premise that unified, coherent, and integrated strategies for the improvement, knitted together into a comprehensive design, will work better than the same strategies implemented in isolation from each other. The federal government's comprehensive school reform program identifies 11 required elements, as follows:

- Proven methods and strategies based on scientifically based research.
- A comprehensive design with aligned components.
- On-going, high-quality professional development for teachers and staff.
- Measurable goals and benchmarks for student achievement.
- Support within the school by teachers, administrators, and staff.
- Support for teachers, administrators, and staff.
- Meaningful parent and community involvement in planning, implementing, and evaluating school improvement activities.
- High-quality technical support and assistance from an external partner with experience and expertise in school-wide reform and improvement.
- Evaluation strategies for the implementation of school reforms and for measurable student results, achieved annually.
- Resources to support and sustain the school's comprehensive reform effort.
- Strategies that have been found to significantly improve the academic achievement of students or that have strong evidence to suggest they will significantly improve the academic achievement of students.

A second school reform approach is to create new schools, either by establishing a new school locally or by adopting an externally developed whole-school model.

The third school reform approach is to create collaborative relationships between the school and outside organizations, such as government agencies and local community organizations. This approach—which can be combined with the other two—is based on the idea that schools do not have the resources or expertise to attend to all the needs of their students and their students' families.

Systemic Approaches

Systemic approaches involve making changes to the entire educational system under the assumptions that such changes can transform how all schools function in the system, what some scholars have labeled "systemic school reform". Systemic effort can occur at the federal, state, or local level of government. One specific systemic reform is to raise the compulsory schooling age—the age to which students must attend school—to eighteen. Another is to change high school graduation requirements, both the number and specific array of courses that students must pass to be awarded a diploma, as well as to specify whether students must pass a high school exit exam to earn a diploma. A third reform is to create alternative pathways or options for completing high school, including dual enrollment programs that allow high school students to take college courses while still in high school, public charter schools, and vouchers that allow students to attend private high schools".

Stimulating Change in "Overstressed" High Schools

The following is a listing of some common practices with a rating of the strength of the evidence of effectiveness, as evaluated by the What Works Clearinghouse and cited in the Rumberger text:

- Utilize data systems that support a realistic diagnosis of the number of students who drop out and that help identify individual students at high risk of dropping out. (level of evidence: low)
- Assign adult advocates to students at risk of dropping out. (level of evidence: moderate)
- Provide academic support and enrichment to improve academic performance. (level of evidence: moderate)
- Implement programs to improve students' classroom behavior and social skills. (level of evidence: low)
- Personalize the learning environment and instructional process. (level of effectiveness: moderate)
- Provide rigorous and relevant instruction to better engage students in learning and provide the skills needed to graduate and to serve them after they leave school. (level of evidence: moderate).

The 2010 plan from the Baltimore City Public Schools, entitled Graduating Great Kids,[5] defines the goals of its comprehensive plan to address the fact that some 5,000 students a year have been dropping out of school in that city. The components are as follows:

- Expand high-quality school options for all youth:
  - Expand early childhood education
  - Expand the availability of specialty settings for youth at risk of dropping out
  - Continue to expand the portfolio of choices for students
- Expand career education and workforce readiness programs in schools:
  - Implement the learning to work initiative
  - Promote the expansion of Career and Technology Education (CTE)
  - Increase the availability of work opportunities, such as internships
  - Expand school-community collaborations
- Align teaching and learning with postsecondary success:
  - Rigorous curriculum and assessment
  - Expand on collaborations that connect youth in high school to college
  - Improve financial literacy
- Develop human capital:
  - Provide teachers with ongoing professional development around student data for early warnings of students at risk
  - Ensure that all teachers are qualified and effective in the classroom
  - Provide schools with the resources and support they need for populations with special circumstances. (i.e., students in foster care, teen parents, homeless youth)
- Develop an effective, district-wide student tracking data system:
  - A centralized method of tracking and reporting student data
  - An early indicator tracking system to identify potential dropouts as early as 3rd grade
  - A student performance system
  - Gather accurate post-secondary data
- Deepen family and community engagement:
  - Family engagement
  - School–community collaboration
  - Engage business and community partners

A document prepared by the Maryland State Department of Education, entitled *Dropout Prevention/School Completion Intervention Resource Guide*,[6] released in 2011, is also referenced the What Works Clearing House (WWC). The clearinghouse publishes intervention reports that evaluate research on school- and community-based dropout prevention curricula and instructional strategies for middle and/or high schools. The following is a listing of the interventions, followed by whether these curricula or programs have or have not "positive or potentially positive effects for at least one improvement outcome."

- Accelerated middle schools:
  - Self-contained academic programs
  - Can help middle school students 1 or 2 years behind grade level to catch up
  - Can be structured as separate schools or as school-within-a-school in a traditional middle school
  Review status showed evidence of positive or potentially positive effects for at least one improvement effort.
- ALAS:
  - An intervention for secondary students focusing on multiple factors that affect dropping out
  - Counselor/mentor monitors attendance, behavior, and academic achievement trains students in problem-solving, self-control, and assertiveness skills
  - Counselor/mentor trains parent in parent–child problem solving, how to participate in school activities, and how to contact leaders and school administrators to address issues
  Review status showed evidence of positive or potentially positive effects for at least one improvement outcome.
- Career academies:
  - School-within-school program
  - Career-related curricula based on career interest, work experience, and coursework
  Review status shows evidence of positive or potentially positive effects for at least one improvement outcome.
- Check and connect:
  - Mentoring program that monitors student engagement through monitoring indicators

- Mentor advocates for student interest

Review status shows evidence of positive or potentially positive effects for at least one improvement outcome.

- Financial incentives for teen parents to stay in school:
  - Encourages teenage parents to go to school and graduate
  - Incentives or sanctions based on participants' performance

Review status shows evidence of positive or potentially positive effects for at least one improvement outcome.

- High school redirection:
  - Alternative high school program for youth at risk for dropping out
  - Teachers serve as mentors and advisors to participants

Review status shows evidence of positive or potentially positive effects for at least one improvement outcome.

- Job Corps:
  - Services students 16–24, typically in a residential program
  - Offers general education diploma (GED) preparation and vocational training

Review status shows evidence of positive or potentially positive effects for at least one improvement outcome.

- National Guard Youth challenge Program:
  - A residential program serving students at-risk
  - Offers GED preparation and life skills training
  - Quasi-military; participants live in barracks, wear uniforms, and follow military discipline

Review status shows evidence of positive or potentially positive effects for at least one improvement outcome.

- Talent development high schools:
  - School reform model that reforms the school's structure and curricula
  - Schools reorganize into smaller learning communities

Review status shows evidence of positive or potentially positive effects for at least one improvement outcome.

For more information on the works and publications of the What Works Clearinghouse, visit http://ies.ed./gov/ncee/wwc/. The What Works Clearinghouse is under the umbrella of the Institute of Education Services, at the US Department of Education, National Center for Education Evaluation and Regional Assistance.

Questions to think about:

1. Have any of the ideas and/or programs you have read about in this chapter led you to think about whether any of them could be adopted in your school or district? If so, which ones are they?
2. If you think of some of the ideas and/or programs listed may be appropriate for your school or district, what can you do, as the DPS, to bring these about?
3. Based on your own knowledge of your school and district, are there other ideas and/or programs that were not mentioned, that you think may be useful for local implementation? If so, what are they?
4. What steps need to be taken to bring these new ideas and programs into your school or district?

Conclusion

I sincerely hope that the material presented in these pages will assist you, as a dropout prevention specialist, to be a catalyst in your school and/or district, in identifying those students, either individually or in groups, who are at risk for dropping out of school. By helping to craft and implement opportunities, services, and supports to address the issues and needs identified in the student body, you are helping tremendously to lower the potential for more students dropping out.

I hope you have come to see that both the causes and possible solutions to the dropout crisis are both numerous and often interrelated. It will take a myriad of strategies to address the issue of the continuing large numbers of students falling by the wayside and failing to graduate from high school. As I read through these documents again, I could not help but notice the commonality among many of the ideas and strategies regarding what needs to be done. I hope that this workbook will give you some renewed passion and direction in addressing the issues that are contributing to the dropout problem.

If I can be of any further assistance to you, please contact me at hblonsky@earthlink.net.

The Dropout Prevention Specialist Workbook. Howard M. Blonsky, Oxford University Press (2020).
© Oxford University Press.
DOI: 10.1093/oso/9780190090845.003.0008

Appendix

Table of Contents

CONTINUUM OF IMPROVED ATTENDANCE
AND ITS RELATIONSHIP TO ACADEMIC PERFORMANCE
AND THE REDUCTION OF DROPOUTS

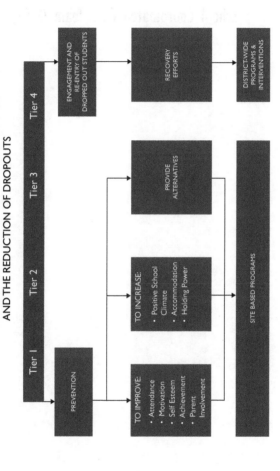

School Coordinated Care Team (SCCT)

SCHOOL COORDINATED CARE TEAM

Frequently Asked Questions

1. Why do we need a Coordinated CARE team at our school?

   CARE teams serve a variety of purposes at the school. They bring together the student services personnel and teachers (whenever possible) in a forum that meets on a regular basis to discuss students of concern, determine the types of intervention assistance these students may receive, to monitor the effectiveness of their efforts, and to do so in a coordinated way. The CARE team also helps to coordinate the community based resources of the school with those provided by the district, and the services and resources of the larger community that may be providing school-based or school-linked services to the school. The CARE team identifies patterns or trends in the needs of students, and assists the administration in advocating for, creating and implementing new programs, services and resources, or alternations in existing programs. In setting a direction for serving individual students, the team makes sure that unique services available in the school, such as the SST process, Section 504, referrals for Special Education assessment, etc., are utilized in the appropriate way for those students who can most benefit from them.

2. When can/does our Coordinated CARE team meet? We are all so busy already?

   It is expected that the CARE team will meet at a regularly scheduled time, at least bi-weekly. It is hoped that an entire morning every other week is reserved for CARE team and Student Success Team (SST) meetings. Hopefully, the schedules of itinerant personnel have been coordinated at the district level so that they can join with the student support personnel stationed at the site, and can all be at the school for this important regular meeting. A typical morning schedule may look something like the following: The CARE team meeting would take place from 8:00 AM until 9:30. Following the CARE team meeting, there will be two to four SST meetings scheduled, each one lasting forty five minutes to one hour. While some student service personnel may leave after the CARE team meeting, others may choose to stay and attend one or more SST meetings, especially if they are familiar with the student, are providing services to the student, or may become involved in providing services to the student.

   It does require a great deal of flexibility by each member of the team to dedicate the necessary time to participate in CARE team and SST and SART meetings. It is believed that this time is very worthwhile, and will prove useful to both students and staff alike. We hope that everyone will make the commitment to regularly attend these meetings, and have the full support of the administration for CARE team members to make this commitment.

3. Who will be on our Coordinated CARE team?

The exact number and roles of the members of the CARE team will vary from site to site. It is expected that the following staff, if available at the school, will serve as regular members of the team:

- Principal, Assistant Principal, or designee
- CARE team facilitator
- Teachers: Referring teacher(s) whenever possible, or a person representing the input of the teacher(s), a peer general education liaison, and a special education liaison.
- School psychologist
- School Social Worker
- Guidance counselor (s)
- Dropout Prevention Specialist (DPS)
- Wellness center staff
- Mental health staff
- Parent liaison
- After school program staff
- A representative from City/County or community-based agencies with whom the school or district has formed partnerships.

4. Who is in charge of the Coordinated CARE team?

There are certain roles that must be assumed by someone, however these roles are/can be fluid, and may be rotated from one person to another such as at the end of a quarter or a semester.The leadership/facilitator/ coordinator function is obviously very important, and the person who assumes this role should be someone who has the trust of the members of the team. The person who assumes this role will receive the Requests for Assistance forms submitted by the referring person(s), prepare the agenda, inform all members of the team as to the time, date and location of the meeting, and make sure that all supporting material will be present for the meeting. The facilitator will also be responsible to keep a CARE team binder that will include the Service/Action plans of students who come before the team, as well as a signed Oath of Confidentiality form from each member of the team. The facilitator will guide the meeting, making sure that the discussion moves forward in a timely way. There must also be a recorder who will record the information decided at the meeting on the Service/Action plan documents, and ensure that the appropriate feedback is provided to the referring person(s). A timekeeper is also an important role for someone to assume, and s/he can help the facilitator to keep the meeting on schedule so that the entire agenda can be covered. From my own experiences, this is not easy to do, but very important.

5. When a student is brought for discussion before the CARE team, what is expected to be brought to the table?

Having the right documentation and materials at the meeting will avoid having to search for information later that a member believes would have helped them to know the student better if this information had been provided. These include:

- The Request for Assistance form
- The cumulative (cum) folder (The person who refers the student to the team, or the guidance counselor, should have reviewed, the cum folder and be able to highlight information that may be relevant, i.e., previous test data, past school history, health/medical issues, contacts with the family, etc.)
- A teacher input form from each of the student's current teachers
- Report cards or scholarship record, attendance record, and any record of disciplinary actions.
- At the elementary level, recent work samples and/or in-class assignments

If the presentation of the student is done in a concise way, the chance for the development of a complete and potentially effective plan will be achieved.

6. Does the Coordinated CARE team structure function the same way at the Elementary, Middle or High School level?

Essentially yes, but with some minor differences as follows. At the elementary level, it may be the referring teacher who presents the student for discussion, or they may do this in partnership with a core member of the school's CARE Team. At the middle school level, it is assumed that teachers have regularly scheduled grade level team meetings, or "academic family" meetings, and this team has "brainstormed" ideas, and tried various interventions on behalf of the student. When a middle school student is brought to the CARE team for discussion, a representative of the teacher(s) team, or the counselor who has met with the student and his/her teachers, will present the student to the other members of the CARE team. Some middle schools will schedule a discussion of students' one grade level at a time, such as the 6th grade team one week, and the 7th grade team the next. In order for the entire grade level team to be present, the meeting may be held before school starts. In this model, both new students and students for follow-up discussion for that grade level would be the first items on the agenda. The other members of the CARE team can continue with the discussion once the classroom teachers have gone to their respective classrooms. At the high school level, it is very difficult to get all teachers to the table at one time, and most often they do not meet in grade level teams. To accommodate this difference, the counselor of the student would present the student to the team, making sure that they have the written input for each of the students' teachers.

7. What types of interventions/accommodations/modifications are typically developed by the CARE team?

Whether at the CARE team, in an SST meeting, or at a meeting of the School Attendance Review Team, the following areas for intervention should be considered:

- Classroom assistance/modifications/accommodations
- Opportunities, services and supports available at the larger school, but not necessarily in each classroom. (i.e., tutoring, mentoring, after school program, etc.)
- Assistance from/with the family
- Utilization of community-based services, programs and resources.

This listing is frequently referred to as the "Broad range of interventions"

8. What would a typical CARE team agenda look like?

Usually, the first item on the agenda is a discussion of individual students who have not come before the team previously. This number may be anywhere from two to six or seven. The second item on the agenda would be a listing of students who have come before the team before, and already have an active Service/Action plan. The purpose of these discussions is to check on the progress of the original plan, or "follow-up", and to make any necessary changes to the plan, as needed, followed by setting a date for the next review/follow-up. The next item on the agenda would be a listing of the SST meetings that are scheduled, so that members of the team who plan to attend these meetings can put the information on their calendars. Following a listing of SSTs scheduled, any program issues can be discussed. This could include a discussion of program or service needs based on trends or issues identified in the student body by disaggregating the academic, attendance and behavioral data. Based on these discussions, the team may decide to develop a proposal and/or apply for a grant, modify a current program or structure in the school, and/or "brainstorm" ideas on how to address what has been learned. The last item on the agenda can list any issues that members of the team want to be placed on the agenda for the next meeting. (A sample agenda follows these Q and A's).

_____School

Coordinated Care Team

Confidentiality Agreement

Program Staff and Extended Team Members

I, the undersigned, hereby agree not to divulge any information or records concerning any name of students, family members, or other individuals of the _____school District community, without proper authorization in accordance with the state and federal law and interagency agreements. I recognize that any discussion of or release of information to any unauthorized person is forbidden and may be grounds for legal and/or other disciplinary action.

During the performance of my assigned duties, I will have access to confidential information required for effective service coordination and delivery. I agree that all discussions, records, and information generated or maintained in connection with these activities will not be disclosed to any unauthorized person.

Confidentiality Agreement:

1. I will comply with confidentiality law and policy as it pertains to securing, orally, sharing, copying or recording confidential information and records of any individuals and families about whom I obtain information.

2. I will restrict requests for access to _____(name of district) and other agencies confidential information and records; and limit sharing of confidential information to those authorized to formulate and implement a case specific service plan as specified in WIC 1989.40 and WIC 1898.45.

I recognize that the unauthorized release of confidential information may expose me to civil/criminal liability and a penalty of $10,000, court costs, and reasonable attorney fees.

Signature: _____date:_____

Print name: _____Job Title: _____

Received by: _____
                Signature of authorized personnel

San Francisco Unified School District

This document is designed for use by SAP/CST/SST members to remind staff of their obligation to not share confidential information unless given written permission. Each member of a SAP/CST/SST team should sign this Oath of Confidentiality before participating in confidential meetings regarding student(s).

Oath of Confidentiality

I, the undersigned, hereby agree not to divulge or share any information or records concerning any San Francisco Unified School District student, other youth, and/or family members of the greater San Francisco community, without the agreement that information shared in the course of my duties be confidential, and shall only be used for the purpose of developing and implementing services to promote the health and development or to reduce the health risks and problems of students in our schools.

I recognize that any improper discussion of, or release of information concerning a participant to any unauthorized person is forbidden. During the performance of my assigned duties, I will have access to confidential information required for student and family assessments, interventions, and service coordination.

I agree that all discussions, deliberations, records, and information generated and maintained in connection with these activities will not be disclosed to any unauthorized persons.

I agree to the above statement regarding confidentiality.

Print Name: _____   Signature: _____

Department/School: _____   Date: _____

Dorchester County Public Schools
Student Success Team (SST)
Teacher Input Form – Secondary

To (Teacher):_____   Date:_____

Re: (Student)_____   From:_____

1. Key Questions:

Check appropriate description:	Always	Usually	Sometimes	Never
Attends class				
Is on time				
Comes to class prepared				
Completes class assignments				
Turns in homework				
Follows directions independently				
Needs help to complete tasks				

2. Grades are: Improving_____   Holding_____   Slipping_____

3. Current grade is: A_____   B_____   C_____   D_____   E_____

4. Behavior: Excellent_____   Satisfactory_____   Inconsistent_____   Unsatisfactory_____

5. Strengths:
_____
_____
_____

6. Areas of Concern:
_____
_____
_____

7. Additional Comments/Recommendation for the Team:
_____
_____
_____

Signature:_____

Thank you for your valuable feedback and cooperation!

Chart 4. Defined Roles for Team Members

Facilitator/ Chairperson*	Recorder	Team Member
Before Meeting: • Coordinates logistics before and after meeting • Notifies team members of meeting time, place, and students scheduled • Ensures parent and student are prepared • Knows available resources and how to access them • Assumes ultimate responsibility for group decisions **During Meeting:** • Knows primary role is to facilitate, not to present information • Stands in front of group • Is accountable for time; appoints timekeeper • Helps recorder take accurate notes • Checks for meaning/ understanding • Encourages comments from all team members by asking, "Any questions?" "Any additions?" • Keeps group focused on task • Asks for specifics, not generalities • Is positive, ensures positive feeling tone, compliments group • Is nonjudgmental, encourages others to be nonjudgmental • Diffuses emotionally charged statements • Sees that the team prioritizes concerns and actions • Helps team find win/win solutions for teacher, student, and parents • Expects accountability for group decisions	• Listens carefully for the key words and ideas to be recorded • Writes the comments on the Student Success Team banner (SST Summary Form) • Organizes the information in the appropriate columns • Does not change the meaning of what was said • Asks for clarification, gets accurate information on the summary • Captures basic ideas • Makes corrections non-defensively • Writes legibly and quickly • Shortens words, abbreviates • Does not concentrate unnecessarily on spelling • Uses colors as a visual aid • Uses circles and arrows to connect related information	• Respects and listens to other individuals • Does not cut other people off or put words in their mouths • Questions any statement he/she feels is not accurate • Helps recorder remain neutral and makes sure ideas are being recorded accurately • Uses facilitative behaviors as needed • Focuses energy on content of the Student Summary • Helps group stay on task • Serves as timekeeper or observer as needed • Comes prepared with information on student • Avoids side conversations • Looks for similarities/discrepancies in the information • Is accountable for agreed-upon actions • Does not make commitments for people who are not present at the meeting • May also copy SST Summary (from the banner) on a small sheet **Student:** • Shares progress, feelings, problems, concerns • Participates in the decision-making process • Receives support and assistance from adults in taking responsibility for change • Assumes responsibility for actions on his/her behalf **Parent:** • Shares familial concerns • Contributes information from home environment • Shares effective and ineffective home interventions • Participates in problem solving • Clarifies questions for staff • Assumes responsibility for actions appropriate for family

School Coordinated Care Team (SDCCT) Agenda

School: _____

Date: _____

A. New Students:

1. _____ 2. _____

2. _____ 4. _____

5. _____ 6. _____

B. Follow-up Students:

1. _____ 2. _____

3. _____ 4. _____

5. _____ 6. _____

7. _____ 8. _____

C. SST's Scheduled:	Location	Date	Time
1. _____	_____	_____	_____
2. _____	_____	_____	_____
3. _____	_____	_____	_____
4. _____	_____	_____	_____
5. _____	_____	_____	_____

D. Program/Service Need/Coordination Issues:

1. _____

2. _____

3. _____

E. Agenda Items for next meeting:

1. _____ 2. _____

BRAINSTORMING: A BROAD RANGE OF INTERVENTIONS
Sample interventions and modifications

The classroom
Use gestures to represent vocabulary terms being taught.
Use "mind maps" and graphic organizers for reading comprehension and writing.
Use positive reinforcements (e.g., use of computer).
Provide assignments that enhance student capabilities and that utilize student strengths.
Use a multi-sensory approach.
Assign classroom responsibilities that build confidence and self esteem.
Use a variety of instructional tools.
Modify the curriculum (e.g., high interest, low vocabulary to encourage reading).
Use visuals instead of written notes to study concepts for exams.
Use reinforcements that are specific to the student's likes.
Provide feedback that is specific and shows a student's growth, no matter how small.

The larger school environment
Make environmental changes (e.g. campus beautification, expressions of cultural diversity).
Increase the means for involvement and participation in activities/clubs, and so forth.
Develop peer-tutoring programs and school-based resiliency programs.
Enhance student and campus safety/security (e.g., conflict resolution programs).
Provide comprehensive health and wellness programs and services.
Initiate a mentoring program.
Give leadership opportunities to students (e.g., crossing guard, office monitor, conflict resolution mediator).
Establish a drop-in homework center.
Provide support for transitions

In and with the student's home
Provide a quiet place to study.
Monitor homework.
Establish incentives, rewards, or consequences.
Secure individual tutoring.
Use extended family relationships as mentors and homework helpers.
Create cultural enrichment opportunities.
Give praise for specific behavior or achievement immediately after it occurs.
Be consistent with consequences each time they are needed. Use consequences that are logical and directly relate to the concerned behavior.
Use all of a child's learning channels when helping the student to review a concept, (for example, in learning a new spelling word, the child sky-writes the word, draws a picture to represent the meaning, creates a song or rhyme or a song using the word, then use it in a sentence).
Purchase toys and games that have an educational value.
Follow through on recommend referrals

In and with the resources of the greater community
Promote partnerships with after school programs; co-locate some on school campuses.
Collect information, such as referral assistance and linkages with the network of resources and services in the community, including those that offer free or reduced cost services, or are based on a sliding scale.
Connect with community centers, boy's and girl's clubs, street work organizations, etc.
Implement and utilize business and community mentoring.
Identify pre-employment and employment opportunities.
Enlist the resources of the faith community.
Learn about and utilize food pantries, clothing exchanges and child watch bartering.
Create bridges to the health, social services and mental health agencies in the community.
Recruit volunteers.

Care Team Referral Form

DREAM SCHOOL Campus: ☐ Drew   ☐ 21ˢᵗ Century   ☐ GRD

San Francisco Unified School District

Scholar (Last, First)	Grade	Advisor	HO Number [leave blank]
Name of Person Making Referral	Title	Tel Ext	Today's Date

Please circle if scholar is receiving any of these services: Special Ed   RSP   AB3632   504

Your concerns about scholar: *(please check and provide descriptive details)*	What have you tried already? *(please check & note key points)*	What interventions do you suggest?
☐ Academic _____ _____ Scores _____ ☐ Attendance (lateness, absence) _____ ☐ Family/home _____ ☐ Emotional or Behavioral _____ ☐ Physical Health/Medical _____ ☐ Other _____ _____	☐ Academic support ☐ Review of cum folder ☐ Confer 1:1 with scholar ☐ Contact with family ☐ Confer with other teachers of this scholar ☐ SART/SARB process ☐ Other	☐ Behavioral contract/incentives ☐ Community program (suggestions?) ☐ Emotional counseling (eg therapist, CBO*) ☐ Enrichment program(s) ☐ Health follow-up ☐ Home visit ☐ Mentoring ☐ Parent/Caregiver follow-up ☐ Peer Resource Program ☐ Scholar Success Team (SST) ☐ Support group: _____ ☐ Translation: _____ ☐ Tutoring during/after school ☐ Other
		*Community Based Organization

===

Care Team Response

Our multidisciplinary team represents counseling, health, parents/caregivers, administration, Beacon & associated programs, mental health, Special Education, and others. We appreciate your making this referral. A Primary Contact Person will follow up by coordinating appropriate services. You will receive a PRELIMINARY response regarding Contact Person and interventions planned.

Date Referral Received	Counselor/Primary Teacher	Primary Contact Person	Others involved:

Concerns	Interventions Planned

ORIGINAL: Care Team Binder   YELLOW COPY: Primary Contact Person   PINK COPY: Referral Source, then returned to CT
Care Team-Dream Schools/September 2005/lbc

SAMPLE
STUDENT ASSISTANCE PROGRAM ACTION FORM

Name of Student _____ HO# _____ Referral Date: _____

Birthdate: _____ Grade: _____ Phone: _____

Lives with _____ Parent(s) _____ Other/Specify Responsible Adult: _____

Home Language: _____ Service Coordinator/Point Person: _____

Current on-Site Services: _____ Community Services: (Contact and Phone No.)

Specify Desired Outcome: Improved Academic Success Attendance Behavior

DATE	ISSUES(S) CONCERN:	INTERVENTION(S) ACTIONS	RESPONSIBLE PERSON	TIMELINE	REVIEW DATE	DID PLAN WORK
1.						
2.						
3.						

Talbot County Public Schools
Coordinated Action Plan

Student's Name:_____ Date:_____

Teacher/Referring Staff:_____ Room:_____

Case Manager/Contact Person:_____

What? *(Action Items)*	Who? *(Person responsible)*	When? *(Date to initiate or complete action item)*	Result
☐ Academic			
☐ After School Program			
☐ Group (e.g. anger management, social skills, grief, etc.)			
☐ Health review & referrals			
☐ Home visit			
☐ Mentoring			
☐ One-to-one counseling/check-ins			
☐ Parent Teacher Conference (documented)			
☐ Tutoring			
☐ Student Success Team (SST)			
☐ Other: (further interventions based on student's needs)			
☐ _____			
☐ _____			
☐ _____			

☐ Copy to Care Team Binder
☐ Copy to Point Person/Contact Person
☐ Copy to Teacher/ Referral Source

Student Success Team (SST) process

STUDENT SUCCESS TEAM (S)

Frequently asked questions

1. What is the practice philosophy of the SST process?

The SST is a strength-based inquiry and "joining" process that brings together the significant people in the life of a student toward the goal of creating a shared plan that hopefully will increase the overall success of the student. The process provides an opportunity for these key individuals to present their insights into the strengths of the student, their concerns, and, through a problem-solving and coordinating process, seeks positive solutions for maximizing the student's potential and success.

The SST process is based upon the belief that the school needs to work in partnership with the student, his/her caregivers, school support staff, and the other child and family resources of the larger community to address obstacles that become evident in the school setting. By drawing together these networks of support, successful intervention(s) can and do occur. The philosophy of the process is saying to the student and family that we can only achieve our shared hopes and goals in partnership with them, not by the school alone making a plan that they do not have involvement in developing and "owning" the plan.

2. When can we find time to schedule SST meetings?

Trying to find a convenient time for both school staff and caregivers to meet can be a real challenge. Many schools schedule SST meetings either before or after school; however, if the meetings are held before school, it is important to allow enough time so that the meeting is not too rushed. At the elementary school level, there may be a time in the day when administrators and support staff are available, (i.e., after recess or after lunch) and when classroom coverage is available to the teacher by a colleague, (i.e., a kindergarten teacher who teaches in the morning may be available in the afternoon). At the secondary level, many schools are moving toward a common "prep", or planning time, for grade level academic teachers to meet. This might be an excellent time to convene an SST meeting if the caregiver(s) are available to meet with all of their student's teachers in an SST format. Some schools have late start times each week to hold special meetings. If it is not possible to find a time for the caregiver to meet with their student's teachers, the grade counselor can represent the input of the teachers, especially if each teacher has completed the Teacher Input form. (A sample of this form is provided following these Q and A's). If the student was referred for an SST meeting by a particular teacher, it is helpful if that teacher can be relieved from their classroom if the meeting is being held during one of their class periods. In this case, in respect to the teachers' time, s/he should be given the opportunity to present their views of the student's strengths, what they have done to be helpful, how it worked, what their concerns are, and any suggestions they have to improve the situation.

In any case, FLEXIBILITY is the key. Those who believe in and support the process are usually able to work out some accommodation that meets the scheduling needs of the majority of the team members. Needless to say, the team member who sets up and schedules the SST meetings has to be a bit of a juggler. **Prioritizing time for SST meetings can, in the long run, reduce the time in addressing these issues later.**

3. Who are the key personnel involved in the SST process?

There are both standing members and student specific members for an SST meeting. The so called "standing members" are the facilitator of the meeting process, a recorder who will record the discussion as it moves along, and hopefully, a general education liaison, especially at the elementary school level. Having a respected general education teacher liaison is particularly important when discussing classroom interventions/modifications, as the other teachers are apt to accept the suggestions of someone who they see as a peer, rather than "support staff personnel" who often serve as facilitators or recorders of the SST. It is also very helpful to have an administrative representative serving as a "core" member of the team. Student specific members of the team are the teacher(s) of the student, the student, the caregivers of the student, other school and/or district level support staff, community agency personnel that may be involved with this student/family, and other significant individuals such as advocates and relatives.

The functions of the "core" members of the team are fluid, and roles can be changed from time to time. Additionally, there can be more than one Student Success Team at the school, such as one team for each grade level, or one for each of the "small learning communities".

4. When should a student be considered for an SST meeting?

Many schools use a "filtering process" that includes interventions/modifications/accommodations at various levels prior to actually scheduling an SST meeting. Examples might include discussions regarding the student at teacher grade level meetings, the grade level counselor and/or school social worker first attempting to address these issues, or the school site CARE team. An SST is often recommended when other assistance has not been successful. A student can also be considered for an SST when it is considered useful to bring the significant people in the life of the student together for discussion and planning. Students can also be referred through the CARE team, directly by their parent/guardian, or by a classroom teacher through the on-site SST facilitator.

In some districts the Student Success Team is utilized as a step prior to referral for a formal assessment and consideration of Special Education services or 504 accommodations. In the past, many have perceived the SST process as a vehicle for expediting students into Special Education. In reality, the SST is intended to assist students in becoming more successful so as to avoid Special Education whenever possible. The SST works with all partners in an attempt to bring this about. The SST should neither be a process to expedite a student to a formal assessment for consideration of Special Education or 504 services, or to serve as a roadblock for such a referral.

5. Why should I refer a student for discussion before the CARE team or an SST meeting?

The purpose of both the CARE team and the SST process is to bring together a group of people who all possess different talents, knowledge and expertise toward the goal of helping the student to become as successful as possible, both academically and socially. The goal is to provide new strategies that address the concerns and tap into the students strengths. It is hoped that each member who sits on one of these teams will contribute their ideas and accept some responsibility for providing some part of the plan that is developed. It is also hoped that the referring person(s) will gain some assistance in addressing their concerns about the student.

6. When are students and parents not appropriate at an SST meeting?

Both students and their caregivers are core members of the SST process. In fact, the SST meeting is not considered a true SST unless these important people are in attendance. Even very young children can participate in at least part of the meeting. It helps to demystify what is going on in the meeting room. Almost all students, regardless of their age, can tell the team what they like about school, what they don'tt like about school, and what things that might make school better for them.

7. Don't students feel overwhelmed when they enter the meeting room and see so many important adults in their life gathered for the SST meeting?

There are two ways to look at this question. Some may feel somewhat overwhelmed and defensive when they first enter the room, knowing that the focus of the meeting is about them, and their progress, or lack of same, in school. On the other hand, when the student sees that a number of important people in his/her life have gathered together on their behalf, a powerful message of caring and commitment to their success is given. Considering that adults all have busy schedules and that they have all found a way to come together on behalf of the student, the importance of the occasion, and the potential importance for the students' future is evident. The student clearly gets this powerful message, even if he or she is not overjoyed at the reason for this meeting at the beginning.

Orientation to the meeting is important for the student and the caregiver(s) as well. It is useful to have a member of the team meet with the student prior to the SST meeting to answer questions about the process and purpose of the SST meeting. During this orientation meeting the student may be asked to complete a brief, open-ended questionnaire about their likes and dislikes regarding school, future goals, and what they would like to see come out of the meeting. When the purpose of the meeting is explained to students, and they hear that they are equal members of the team, that their input is welcomed and necessary, most students respond positively.

8. As a facilitator, how do I handle confidential issues that may arise during the SST meeting?
The facilitator must be careful in handling confidential or other sensitive issues that may emerge in the SST meeting. It is best to look at both verbal and nonverbal cues from parent/guardian and/or student to determine whether or not they are comfortable in pursuing a particular discussion in front of the team gathered for the meeting. At times, it is useful to designate a member of the team who will meet with the student or parent/guardian individually to discuss these issues. This separate meeting then becomes an action item listed in the SST Summary form, which is often referred to as the "group memory".

REQUEST FOR STUDENT SUCCESS TEAM MEETING

Date referral received: _____

Student _____ Birthdate _____

Address _____ Home phone _____

Parent _____ Work phone _____

Grade _____ Teacher _____ Room # _____

Student receiving: Chapter I _____ ELD _____ Speech _____ Counseling _____

Attendance: Days Absent _____ Excused _____ Unexcused _____ Tardies _____

Circle retention grade: **K** **1** **2** **3** **4** **5** **6** **7** **8**

Significant health concerns _____

_____

Test Scores: Date _____ Reading _____ Language _____ Math _____

Proficiencies _____

Referred to SST by: _____ Position: _____

Describe your specific academic and non-academic concerns regarding this student:

_____

_____

_____

Have you met with the parent to discuss your concerns and explain the Student Success Team process? _____

Method: _____ Dates: _____

Results of parent contact: _____

_____

_____

_____

SST Meeting scheduled:

Date: _____ Room: _____

Time _____

Preparation Checklist for SST Meeting

Review the student's cum folder and other records, paying particular attention to:

* History of standardized achievement test data
* Current and past attendance and tardy information
* Hearing and vision screening results, health issues
* Past school history, including retention and referral to other programs
* Relevant history of contacts with caregivers

Be prepared to present specific background information about the student, including:

* **Strengths** (to be built upon for developing interventions and modifications)
      Academic (e.g., good with math problem-solving, likes to read, enjoys art and exceptional science project.
      Social/Emotional (e.g., wants to please adults, chosen by classmates as a friend and/or as a leader).
      Multiple Intelligence characteristics: linguistic, logical-mathematical, bodily-kinesthetic, spatial, musical, interpersonal, intrapersonal.
* **Interests:** (including student preferences for reading and writing topics, science and math themes, projects, etc.)
* **Academic functioning** in reading, oral language, written language and math (bring any curriculum-based data to show levels).
* Amount and quality of class work and homework (bring recent work samples).

Be ready to discuss:

* Your basic concern or concerns (academic, behavior, social-emotional, health, etc.)
* Desired student outcomes (the improvements you would like to see as outcomes), such as better attendance, increase in reading or math skills, improved ability to work with/get along with peers, ability to follow classroom or playground rules.
* Strategies and modifications you have tried, and their results.
* Efforts to work with the caregivers to resolve your concerns.

Bring to the SST meeting:

* Student's cumulative file **(Guidance Counselor)**
* Recent work samples that reflect both strengths and areas of concern.
* In-class assessments which show academic levels in Content and Performance standards.

Student Success Team (SST) Best Practices Checklist

Pre SST Meeting:

* There is a designated person who coordinates the SST process.
* There is a referral process in place that uses the Request for Assistance form along with other documentation provided from Levels I and II.
* Staff is aware of the SST process and knows who the SST Coordinator is.
* Core members of the SS Team need to be identified. These people will most often attend all SST meetings and the roles that they assume, (facilitator, recorder, time keeper, etc.) are fluid and interchangeable.
* The parent/caregiver receives a meeting notice and the SST Parent Brochure in their home language and in a timely manner.
* A member if the team assumes responsibility to "outreach" to the caregiver, to discuss the purpose of the meeting, and to address any barriers to their attendance. While the brochure is a good overview for families, it cannot take the place of personal contact, encouragement, and assistance when needed. This is often an important first step in developing a working relationship with the caregiver.
* If a referring teacher will be attending the SST meeting, the teacher receives the Teacher Preparation Checklist prior to the SST meeting.
* The student is prepared for what to expect in the SST meeting, and given an opportunity to clarify any questions.
* The SST chair or coordinator should make necessary arrangements, including that a room is available, all participants are notified as to time and place, roles are defined in advance, relevant material is available at each meeting (i.e., cum folder, scholarship record, test scores, attendance, etc.) and the SST wall chart posted

During the SST Meeting:

* Team members are consistent in attending the meeting.
* An interpreter/translator is provided (when the language of the home is not English).
* Meetings start and end on time (30-60 minutes for an initial SST, 15-45 minutes for a follow-up meeting).
* The facilitator welcomes the caregiver, allows for introductions of those gathered, and explains the purpose and process of the SST meeting. Special attention should be given to addressing the student, explaining that this meeting is for and about them, but not something being done to them, rather with them, and that their input and agreements are most welcome.
* There are designated people who fulfill roles during the meeting (e.g., facilitator, recorder, team member, etc.).
* Members participate and share their respective knowledge.
* It is very important to start the meeting with student strengths. It sets a positive tone for the meeting, and gives everyone an opportunity to be heard, this setting the stage for equal input and respectful listening.
* The facilitator should guide the meeting along, being mindful of the time, the

importance of covering each column topic, and keeping the tone positive.

* SST Summary Form and/or the SST Follow-up Form is used to document the meeting and serves as a guide for meeting discussion. If using the wall chart, the relevant information should be transferred to the 8 ½" x 14"format after the meeting to insure a permanent record.

* The team should brainstorm a "broad range of interventions" (classroom, larger school, home and community) for each student discussion.

* Action items should be selected from the list of "brainstormed" ideas, responsibility for each item is assigned, and a date set for when implementation will begin.

* All participants should sign at bottom of the SST Summary or SST Follow-up meeting form. The signature of the parent/guardian/caregiver stating that they agree with the plan gives authority to move forward with what was decided.

* A follow-up meeting is scheduled at the conclusion of the first meeting.

Post SST Meeting:

* Completed SST Summary forms are copied (either first meeting or follow-up) and distributed. (Distribution: a copy to the caregiver, a copy for the teacher, a copy for the cum folder, and a copy for the student's SST file).

* A record of the meeting is entered onto the SST log form that will be kept by the SST coordinator and due each semester to the Office of Student Services.

* Action items are monitored and follow-through occurs. This is crucial if any real change is to occur.

* Members of the original SST are reminded of scheduled follow-up meetings.

Dear Parents and Guardians:

We know students are most successful when there is a cooperative effort between parents and school personnel. In a spirit of shared responsibility, the Student Success Team meets at school, exploring and problem solving, in order to help students. Parents and students are an important part of this team.

What is the student success team? The Student Success Team (SST) is a process of regular education. The team reviews individual student's concerns and plans ways of handling those concerns in the regular classroom.

How is a student selected to be discussed at the SST? Usually the classroom teacher (or the principal) indicates that the student's learning and/or emotional needs are not being adequately met under existing circumstances. Parents may also request an SST if they have a concern.

Will anything have been done to help a child before the SST? Yes, usually the teacher has already made some modifications in the classroom. then the principal and teacher meet to review the student's progress and make additional modifications as necessary.

What does "program modification" mean? Program modifications are measures taken to accommodate special needs. Some examples of modifications are:
- change of seating resulting from vision and hearing screening
- use of diagnostic materials
- visual/auditory aids in giving instruction
- cross-age tutors
- notebooks for assignments
- change of group
- additional lab time
- counseling services
- additional health services and referral

How many people will be at the SST? The team will always include parents, the teacher, the teacher referring the student to the SST, and sufficient staff to review the student's needs.

Are there any other staff members who might be present? Other staff who might be present are: Resource Specialist, Psychologist, Speech and Language Specialist, School Nurse, Counselor, and other specialists.

We look forward to meeting with you to develop a program that will meet the needs of your child.

Our SST meeting for _____ will be held:

Date: _____   Time: _____

Location: _____

Sincerely,

_____   _____
Teacher   Principal

STUDENT SUCCESS TEAM

SST

Parents • School • Community

Parent Brochure

(Name & address of School)

Parent Preparation Questionnaire

My child's strengths are (interests, hobbies, skills): _____

Concerns for my child are: _____

What motivates my child is: _____

Expectations I have for my child are: _____

Student Questionnaire

My strengths are: _____

Things I like about school are: _____

My concerns are: _____

At Home

Ways my family helps me: _____

My Future

When I finish high school I want to _____

Jobs I would enjoy are: _____

What is the Future?

At the end of the meeting, a follow up date will be scheduled to review progress. You will be invited to meet again with members of the SST to evaluate changes and growth in your student.

Additional testing through Special Education resources may be recommended at this time. This recommendation comes from the members of the SST only after modifications and suggestions have not proven to be successful.

What is the Role of the Parent in the SST Process?

The parent:

- provides valuable information and another viewpoint for planning an effective program,

- shares the child's strengths and concerns with school staff,

- participates in the development of a positive intervention plan for their child.

Student Success Team

What is the Student Success Team (SST)?

Students are most successful where there is a strong spirit of cooperation between home and school.

Based on our shared responsibility, the SST meets at school to explore possibilities and strategies that will best meet the educational needs of your student.

How does it Work?

The Process:

Students are typically referred by the classroom teacher, but any member of the school staff may request support from the SST for a student whose learning, behavior or emotional needs are not being met under existing circumstances.

Prior to the first formal SST meeting, teachers have met to review classroom modifications that enhance learning for students. A modification may be as simple as a change in seating location, a daily assignment sheet, or an increase in the use of visual teaching aids. Sometimes a simple change can make a big difference for a student.

Any modification that has been tried or is currently in place will be discussed with you at the SST meeting. Using this information, the team can suggest further steps to help the student.

The Student Success Team Meeting:

Staff members will come prepared with information about your student. Information may include work samples, attendance records or assessment results. All information will be listed on the **SST Summary Form.**

The SST Summary will contain areas of:

- Student Strengths
- Information
- Modifications
- Areas of Concern
- Questions
- Strategies
- Action
- Responsible Person(s)

Other members of the team may include support staff such as: a nurse or psychologist and a meeting facilitator.

B. Use of the SST Header and Banner to Develop the Group Memory

The Header and Banner

The "header banner" is a 6-½ ft. by 1 ft. plastic-coated rolled chart on which the headings for the elements of the SST process have been pre-printed. These SST header charts are available (in both English and Spanish) through the California Department of Education's CDE Press for less than $10 each. Typically, this banner is placed on the wall facing all the SST members. Blank butcher paper is then placed *below* the header and is referred to as the "banner." The **Recorder** lists the comments made by team members on the banner, lining them up underneath the appropriate titles of the header. These comments constitute the group memory. At the meeting the comments are transcribed onto legal-sized paper by a team member.

- The combination of the 6-½ ft. header and butcher paper underneath is used as a focus to structure the communication process during the SST meeting. By recording the group memory onto the banner, under the header, the team develops a clear picture of the student. Even a person who does not know the student at the start of the meeting will see a "picture" of the student emerge as the banner is completed.

- The "banner" provides a place to document the team's positive intervention plan. The information from the banner is transcribed at the meeting and duplicated for all parties participating in the action plan at the end of the meeting.

The SST header is a road map, a sequential agenda that, if followed exactly, provides both a natural and positive flow to the SST meeting and a complete record the discussion. Since this is a positive, strength-based inquiry, the "strengths" section comes first. Proceeding through relevant information headlined in the header often has the effect of illuminating the nature and complexity of a student's concerns effecting his or her school experience. No section should be ignored or given too much emphasis.

Examples of completed SST summaries with information from the banner are in *Forms and Tools*.

The header and banner shown below look like this.

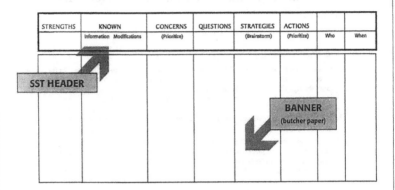

STRENGTHS	KNOWN		CONCERNS	QUESTIONS	STRATEGIES	ACTIONS		
	Information	Modifications	(Prioritize)		(Brainstorm)	(Prioritize)	Who	When

The **banner elements**, as highlighted by the **header**, should be completed fully and are defined as follows:

1. **Strengths Column**

The most important element of the SST process is provided in the column of information indicating the student's strengths. This column should list the student's strengths in all settings – home, community, and school. It should also include what the student sees as his or her strengths and interests. Academic, social, and physical strengths, the student's incentives, and career interests should all be listed. Examples may include the subjects the student likes – leadership ability, hobbies, learning styles, and so forth. The more specific the strength, the better. Rather than say, "Sam is a nice boy," a team member might say, "Yesterday Sam helped other students with their math. He does this often."

The team should identify character strengths particularly, and not stop at references to appearance or athletic ability. If the team is to build on a student's strengths, the strengths identified should be potential building blocks for change.

We must be reminded often that "a student's strengths, in excess, are often his or her stumbling blocks," and vice versa. Many times a teacher's concerns with a student can get in the way of seeing the student's strengths. Strengths often can be found by reframing some of the concerns; for example, "The student talks back" can be reframed as "The student stands up for himself." The concern then becomes how to teach the student to stand up for himself or herself in an appropriate way. *The action plan interventions should be based on the student's strengths.*

Chart 5. Finding Students' Strengths from Their Stumbling Blocks lists some common student strengths that can be recognized in the complaints teachers and others make about students.

2. Known: Information/Modifications Column

Known - Information: All pertinent information regarding the student should be listed in the "KNOWN" Information column. Basic vision and hearing data and other relevant medical information should be listed here. Basic academic levels, attendance, family composition and history, and events happening at home may be relevant to the student's situation.

KNOWN - Modifications: Previous modifications/interventions are outlined in the "KNOWN" Modifications column. The team rates the effectiveness of these modifications with a "+" for effective or a "-" for little or no effect. Examples might include a schedule change, positive behavior contract, counseling, peer tutoring, modifications of assignments, and so forth.

Particularly sensitive or embarrassing information might be shared after the student has been asked to step outside. However, sensitive information should not be used as a reason to exclude the student from the meeting, because it can be rescheduled. The team should exercise care in dealing with material that the parent feels is relevant but not necessarily appropriate for the child to hear. Ultimately, the parents decide if and when a student should be excused temporarily while a sensitive matter is discussed. *(See Including Parents as Team Members and Including Students as Team Members, which appear earlier in this chapter.)*

3. Concerns Column

As mentioned earlier, schools must remember "the problem is the problem," not the student or the family. Some schools have reclassified the concern element as "the obstacle" that needs to be overcome for the student to be successful. The Student Success Team lists the concerns presenting the obstacle(s) that generated the SST referral of the student and prioritizes them in this column. Any academic, social/emotional, physical, or attendance concern may be addressed. These concerns should be specifically stated. For example, rather than saying a student is a "truant," an attendance concern may be written as "The student has missed 15 of the last 25 days of school, unexcused." Caution should be taken not to label the student but to list the observable behavior. The team should limit concerns to the most pressing ones, usually three or four. Then the team should prioritize numerically which concern the team will address first, second, and so forth.

4. Questions Column

This column allows the entire team to voice questions related to the discussion. This is a time to clarify issues and to note those questions or issues that may need to be revisited. New information stated during this time may be recorded during the meeting (add to action plan).

5. Strategies Column (Brainstorm)

At this point in the meeting, *the entire team looks back at the student's strengths to help brainstorm strategies that address the student's concerns.* The team makes no evaluations of the strategies shared at this time. Once listed, the strategies/interventions are typically grouped into four categories: interventions that occur in the classroom, interventions that occur in the larger school environment, strategies that are used in the home, and interventions that occur with the assistance of the larger community. *Chart 6. Brainstorming: A Broad Range of Interventions* provides information on sample interventions that may occur in each of the four categories.

One of the most critical elements in the SST process is brainstorming strategies. Schools must develop a wide range of interventions and resources based on the unique needs of the students they serve.

Remember the four rules for brainstorming:

1. The more ideas you develop, the better.

2. The wilder ideas you discover, the better.

3. You can find opportunities to "hitchhike" by building other ideas.

4. You must wait until later to ask questions, elaborate, or evaluate.

The whole idea is to relax the censor inside the mind so that the creative thinking can run free. Have fun! Brainstormed ideas need to be converted from writing into action. You will have a chance later to discuss, adjust, edit, and decide.

Use the brainstorm list for action planning.

- Look over the list.

- Select the ideas that emerge from the list that seem workable.

- Combine the ideas if you wish.

- Prioritize and select actions.

- When brainstorming, keep a student's strengths in mind.

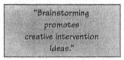

"Brainstorming promotes creative intervention ideas."

Note: If the same concerns occur frequently in this portion of the SST for many students, for example, "student is not turning in homework," the administration needs to consider a *systemic change*, such as providing a homework center.

6. **Actions Column**

This column is the place for developing an "action plan" which is really the prescriptive plan for improvement. It details the responsibilities to be assumed by the teacher, parent, student and community resource persons. It should be reasonable and reflect a positive, supportive effort to restore the student to a successful school experience. For example, "to do homework" is a *goal*, not an *action* item. An *action* item is what the SST recommends to support and assist the student in doing his or her homework; for example, use a school homework center, turn off the TV, create a separate area at home for doing homework, and so forth.

a. **Actions**

The team prioritizes the list of strategies/interventions and selects *new* actions that have the most potential for success, based on the student's strengths, and that address the concerns. These actions should be shared equally by student, family, school, and, when appropriate, by community resource personnel. In no circumstance should the actions listed here be phrased to suggest blame or to place sole responsibility for action on the student and parent.

b. **Who**

A specific person(s) is listed as a responsible party for implementing an action. *Individuals not in attendance at the SST meeting should not be given responsibility for an action.* However, a team member at the meeting may list as an action that he or she will request the assistance of a person not at the meeting. The actions reflect a combined responsibility of the school, parent, student, and community.

c. **When**

A specific date of initiation of any new action is listed in this column. In most instances this is done by suggesting an actual date; for example, February 23, 2000. If determining an exact date is not possible because a referral to a service needs to be completed first and if that service date is not available at the time of the meeting, the date may be listed as "by (future date)." Indeterminate dates, even if they sound immediate, should be avoided, such as "ASAP," "immediately," or "ongoing."

> "Action plan interventions are based on student strengths."

7. **Summary Protocol**

At the bottom of the SST Summary Form are a number of items to be completed before the meeting ends. Examples of blank and completed SST summary forms are included in *Forms and Tools* and on the CD that accompanies this publication. These required actions are listed as follows:

a. **Follow-up Date**

The team agrees to a specific follow-up date and time prior to ending the meeting and writes them on the summary protocol. *Setting up a specific date increases accountability.* The suggested time for a follow-up meeting should be about six to eight weeks. Schools on year-round schedules should try to meet before to the student goes "off track."

b. **Invite**

Any new people to invite are listed in this section. A copy of the initial meeting summary should be given to these individuals prior to the follow-up meeting.

c. **Team Member's Signature/Position**

All SST participants should sign in the signature section of the SST Summary Form. This is a legal document and, as such, should reflect the agreement of all those members present at the meeting. It further sends the message to all present that actions that are planned should be carried out. Also, it adds gravity and importance to what was discussed and decided at the meeting. These signatures help in ensuring accountability for the action plan developed. California *Education Code* Section 54726 requires that significant players, student and parent, student's teacher, and administrator/designee to attend.

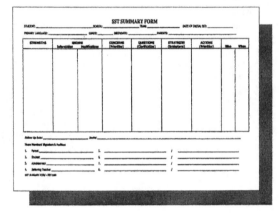

SST Facilitator Observation Checklist

Task	Observations
For all meetings	
The process was kept moving in a timely manner	
The purpose and process of the SST meeting were clearly stated at the beginning	
Student Strengths was the first agenda item discussed	
The caregiver's input was sought within the first ten minutes	
The student's input was sought within the first ten minutes	
Areas of Concern were prioritized and discussed	
All agenda items were discussed	
Curricular and instructional strategies were discussed, including suggestions for modification	
A broad range of interventions was considered: classroom, school/district, home, and community	
Caregiver and student input were solicited in action planning	
Student strengths were considered when selecting interventions	
Responsibility for each Action Item was assigned (with completion date)	
Specific objectives and methods of measuring progress were defined in the action plan	
The facilitator read the Action Items to insure consensus	
A Follow-up meeting date was set	
Team members signed the Meeting Summary form (2.0 or 2.0A) and the caregiver received a copy	
For follow-up SST meetings	
The SST facilitator checked with each team member regarding implementation of agreed upon Action Items from the previous meeting	
New information was discussed	
New concerns were discussed, if appropriate	
The progress toward each Desired Student Outcome was considered in relation to the relevant benchmarks	
A new action plan was devised, if appropriate	

Chart 5. FINDING STUDENTS' STRENGTHS FROM THEIR STUMBLING BLOCKS

Stumbling Blocks	Strengths
These common complaints ➔	can be Indicators of these strengths
Is conceited; cocky	Has confidence
Is inflexible, closed-minded, rigid	Is consistent, shows discipline
Compromises, lacks initiative	Is cooperative
Demonstrates recklessness	Has courage
Is willful	Demonstrates decisiveness
Has a one-track mind	Shows diligence
Is a perfectionist	Shows care and efficiency
Shouts out/talks out of turn/is assertive	Demonstrates enthusiasm
Work is too wordy	Shows expressiveness
Is indecisive, lacks commitment	Indicates fair-mindedness/can see both sides
Is wishy-washy	Is flexible
Shows weakness, is weak-willed	Shows forgiveness
Is tactless, insensitive, undiplomatic	Demonstrates frankness, honesty
Is stingy, penny-pinching, cheap	Shows frugality
Is extravagant, squanders	Is generous
Is outspoken, blunt	Shows honesty
Lacks self-confidence, is timid	Demonstrates humility
Shows blind obedience, mindless servility	Is loyal
Is obsessive/compulsive, a perfectionist	Shows organization, neatness
Is stubborn, headstrong	Shows persistence
Is manipulative, uses high pressure	Demonstrates persuasiveness
Is fraudulent or underhanded	Is resourceful
Seems thin-skinned, oversensitive	Shows sensitivity

Appendix

SST SUMMARY FORM

STUDENT: _____ SCHOOL: _____ TEAM: _____ DATE OF INITIAL SST: _____

PRIMARY LANGUAGE: _____ GRADE: _____ BIRTHDATE: _____ PARENTS: _____

STRENGTHS	KNOWN		CONCERNS Prioritize	QUESTIONS	STRATEGIES Brainstorm	ACTIONS (Prioritize)	Who	When
	Information	Modifications						

Follow Up Date: _____   Invite: _____

Team Members' Signature & Position:

1. Parent _____
2. Student _____
3. Administrator _____
4. Referring Teacher _____

5. _____
6. _____
7. _____
8. _____

Dorchester County Public Schools

Student Success Team
Action Plan/Summary Form

Meeting Date _____

| Student |
| Birthdate   Grade |
| School |
| Teacher/Referral Source |

STRENGTHS
KNOWN INFORMATION (Summarize pertinent student information, e.g. health/developmental status, testing data, work samples)
PRIOR INTERVENTIONS (Include current services, information, modifications, length of time tried & outcome)
AREAS OF CONCERN (Priorities)

DESIRED STUDENT OUTCOMES (Use Menu of Interventions)	AS EVIDENCED BY (Method of progress monitoring)

BRAINSTORMING		

ACTION ITEMS	WHO	WHEN

Follow-up Meeting Date _____ (schedule within 2-6 weeks)

I (parent/caregiver) _____have participated in this action plan

Student	Date	Administrator	Date	Referring Teacher	D
Signature		Signature		Signature	

SST SUMMARY FORM

STUDENT: Lorena Lopez SCHOOL: Clearwater GRADE: 7 BIRTHDATE: 1/25/85 TEAM: "SST3" DATE OF INITIAL SST: March 31, 1997

PRIMARY LANGUAGE: English PARENTS: Navidad & Jorge Lopez

STRENGTHS	KNOWN Information	Modifications	CONCERNS Prioritize	QUESTIONS	STRATEGIES Brainstorm	ACTIONS (Prioritize)	Who	When
Great dancer	Family- Lives with mom and 13-yr-old brother	+ one-to-one tutor for English	Not staying on task - talking ②	Does she have a hearing problem?	1-Counseling at church	Counseling at church	Mom and student	By 4/15
Break dancer		+ met with mom						
POP		- seat change			1-Time-out place in class	Counseling will contact home	Counselor	By 4/30
Likes science	School- 3 elementary schools	- suspended 3 times	Verbal conflicts with some peers and some staff ①	An auditory processing problem?				
Good attendance		+ Saturday school			2-summer school	Teacher will set up	Teacher	By 4/12
Supportive family		+ Uncle helping with math			2-homework center			
Likes to read	Grades- Soc. Studies-D English-F Math-D PE-C		Academics - falling behind, especially English Comprehension weak ③	Does she need glasses	2- Daily planner	Student will purchase and use	Student	By 4/12
Risk taker								
Enjoys helping young children					2-re-check vision and hearing	Mom will set up appointment	Mom	By 4/12
Works hard	Health- Glasses in 4th grade. Ear aches as a child Normal birth Physical 3 years ago				2-quiet place to work with aunt at home	Mom and aunt will help set up	Mom	By 4/30
					2-library card	Dad		

Example of an Exemplary SST Summary Form

Follow Up Date: May 15, 1997 Invite: both mom and dad and aunt.

Team Members' Signature & Position:

1. Parent _____ Navidad Lopez _____   5. _____ Guilda Lowenstein _____ / _____ Teacher
2. Student _____ Lorena Lopez _____   6. _____ Mel Jurisch _____ / _____ ORC
3. Administrator _____ Michelle Allen _____   7. _____ Belinda Guterrez _____ /
4. Referring Teacher _____ Barney Schorr _____   8. _____ Nurse _____ /

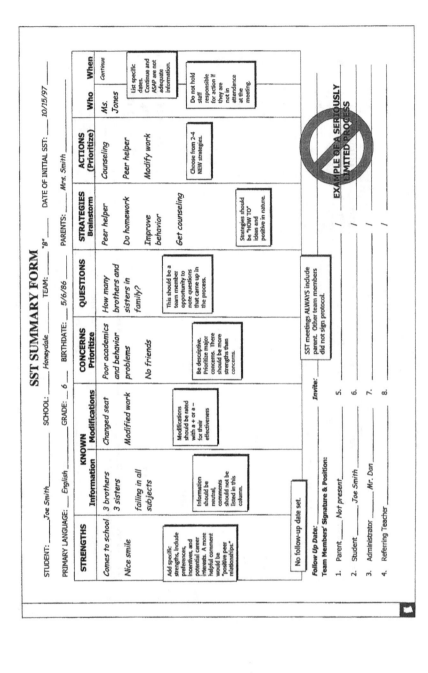

SST SUMMARY FORM

STUDENT: _Joe Smith_   SCHOOL: _Honeydale_   "B"   DATE OF INITIAL SST: _10/15/97_

PRIMARY LANGUAGE: _English_   GRADE: _6_   BIRTHDATE: _5/6/86_   TEAM: PARENTS: _Mrs. Smith_

STRENGTHS	KNOWN Information	KNOWN Modifications	CONCERNS Prioritize	QUESTIONS	STRATEGIES Brainstorm	ACTIONS (Prioritize)	Who	When
Comes to school	3 brothers 3 sisters	Changed seat	Poor academics and behavior problems	How many brothers and sisters in family?	Peer helper	Counseling	Ms. Jones	Continue
Nice smile	failing in all subjects	Modified work	No friends		Do homework	Peer helper		
					Improve behavior	Modify work		
					Get counseling			

Add specific strengths, include preferences, potential career interests. A more helpful comment would be "positive peer relationships."

Information should be neutral, comments should not be listed in this column.

Modifications should be rated with a + or a – for their effectiveness.

Be descriptive. Prioritize major concerns. There should be more strengths than concerns.

This should be a team member opportunity to note questions that came up in the process.

Strategies should be "HOW TO" ideas and positive in nature.

Choose from 2-4 NEW strategies.

list specific dates. Continue and ASAP are not adequate information.

Do not hold staff responsible for action if they are not in attendance at the meeting.

No follow-up date set.

SST meetings ALWAYS include parent. Other team members did not sign protocol.

Follow Up Date: _____   **Invite:**

Team Members' Signature & Position:

1. Parent _____ Not present _____   5. _____
2. Student _____ Joe Smith _____   6. _____
3. Administrator _____ Mr. Don _____   7. _____
4. Refering Teacher _____   8. _____

EXAMPLE OF A SERIOUSLY LIMITED PROCESS

SST FOLLOW UP FORM

STUDENT: _____ SCHOOL: _____ TEAM: _____ DATE OF INITIAL SST: _____

PRIMARY LANGUAGE: _____ GRADE: _____ BIRTHDATE: _____ PARENTS: _____

NEW INFORMATION	PREVIOUS ACTIONS	OUTCOMES	NEW ACTIONS	Who	When

Follow-up Date: _____ *Invite:* _____

Team Members' Signature & Position:

1. Parent _____
2. Student _____
3. Administrator _____
4. Referring Teacher _____

5. _____ / _____
6. _____ / _____
7. _____ / _____
8. _____ / _____

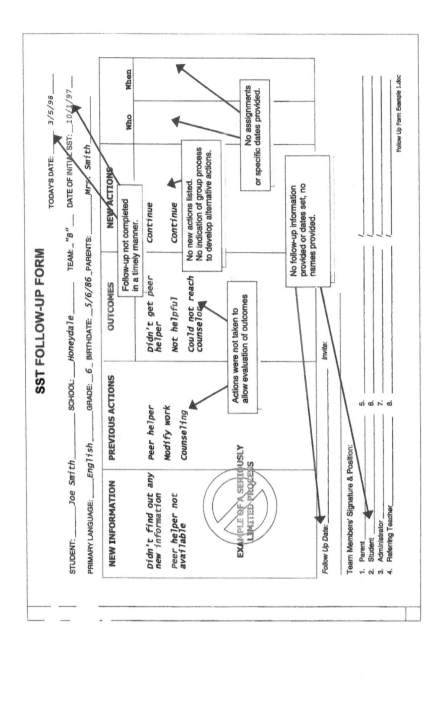

SST FOLLOW-UP FORM

STUDENT: _____Joe Smith_____ SCHOOL: ___Honeydale____ TEAM: _"B"___ TODAY'S DATE: ___3/5/98___

PRIMARY LANGUAGE: ___English___ GRADE: _6_ BIRTHDATE: _5/6/86_ PARENTS: ___Mrs. Smith___ DATE OF INITIAL SST: _10/1/97_

NEW INFORMATION	PREVIOUS ACTIONS	OUTCOMES	NEW ACTIONS		
				Who	When

NEW INFORMATION

Didn't find out any
new information

Peer helper not
available

PREVIOUS ACTIONS

Peer helper

Modify work

Counseling

OUTCOMES

Didn't get peer
helper

Not helpful

Could not reach
counselor

NEW ACTIONS

Continue

Continue

Follow-up not completed
in a timely manner.

No new actions listed.
No indication of group process
to develop alternative actions.

No assignments
or specific dates provided.

Actions were not taken to
allow evaluation of outcomes

No follow-up information
provided or dates set, no
names provided.

EXAMPLE OF A SERIOUSLY
LIMITED PROCESS

Follow Up Date: _____   Invite: _____

Team Members' Signature & Position:

1. Parent _____   5. _____
2. Student _____   6. _____
3. Administrator _____   7. _____
4. Referring Teacher _____   8. _____

Estimados Padres:

Todos sabemos que los estudiantes tienen más éxito en la Escuela cuando los padres y maestros trabajan juntos. En el espíritu de compartir la responsabilidad de la Educación, tenemos un equipo de maestros que se reúnen a estudiar los problemas de aprendizaje y a buscar soluciones para ayudar a los estudiantes. A este equipo lo llamamos **Student Success Team (SST)** Los padres y estudiantes son muy importantes en este estudio.

¿Qué es The Student Success Team? El SST es un proceso de educación regular. El equipo revisa las necesidades personales del estudiante, tomando en cuenta las informaciones que aportan los padres, sus preocupaciones y las habilidades especiales de los estudiantes. El equipo estudia soluciones que se pueden aplicar en la clase regular.

¿Cómo se seleccionan los estudiantes para discutir su caso en el SST? Generalmente los estudiantes son referidos por su maestro (o la Directora) cuando se considera que el estudiante no está alcanzando el nivel adecuado de aprendizaje o desarrollo emocional en las circustancias normales. Los padres también pueden pedir un estudio de SST si tienen alguna preocupación acerca de su estudiante.

¿Qué se ha hecho antes de llamar a un SST? Antes de llamar a esta junta de maestros, se han hecho los cambios apropiados para resolver el problema en la clase del estudiante. La maestra y la directora se han reunido para modificar el programa y revisar los progresos del estudiante.

¿ Qué significa modificar el programa? Significa tomar algunas medidas para acomodarse a las necesidades especiales del alumno; por ejemplo:
- Cambio de asiento si se descubre que el estudiante no ve o no oye bien.
- Uso de materiales especiales; auditivos o visuales para enseñarle.
- Tutores personales para ayuda escolar.
- Uso de cuadernos para tareas.
- Cambio de su grupo de estudio.
- Tiempo adicional para sus laboratorios.
- Servicio de consejeros, salud y referencia a otros servicios.

¿Cuántas personas estarán en la reunión de SST? El equipo siempre incluirá a los padres del estudiante, su maestro, la persona que llamó a la reunión y personal necesario para revisar las necesidades del estudiante.

¿Hay otras personas que estarán presentes? Otras personas que podrán estar presentes son: Maestros de recursos, Psicólogo, Especialista del habla y de aprendizaje, Enfermera de la Escuela, Consejero y otros especialistas.

Esperamos reunirnos con usted para desarrollar un programa que esté de acuerdo con las necesidades de su estudiante.

Nuestro SST para _____

será: Fecha_____   Hora_____

        Lugar_____

Sinceramente,

_____   _____
Maestro   Directora

Bilingual Interview/Teacher _____

Person Interviewed _____

SST REFERRAL ADDENDUM:
Critical Issues for English Language Learning Students

Name _____ Date _____

Grade _____ Birthdate _____

Results of parent contact (include dates): _____
_____
_____

1. Primary Language _____ Dominant Language _____

2. Year in U.S. _____ Country of Birth _____

3. Pupil's language with: parents _____
                             siblings _____
                             peers _____

   Comments _____
   _____

4. Language Dominance
   Test used: (current testing) _____ Date _____

   Test used: _____ Date _____

   Dominant Language: Level: _____
                         LEP: NES _____ LES _____ FES _____
                         FEP: _____
                         Test Used: _____
   Date _____   Level: _____
                         LEP: NES _____ LES _____ FES _____
                         FEP: _____

5. Total years of formal instruction: In U.S. _____ In native country _____

6. Number of schools attended in U.S. _____

7. Attendance: Regular _____   Irregular _____
   Comments _____

8. Language/Instructional programs and services by grade level (circle X):

English only	Pre K	K	1	2	3	4	5	6	7	8
Bilingual	Pre K	K	1	2	3	4	5	6	7	8
BILP	Pre K	K	1	2	3	4	5	6	7	8
ELD	Pre K	K	1	2	3	4	5	6	7	8

Primary reading instructor: Bilingual Teacher _____   Waivered Teacher _____   Aide _____

Problems/Comments: _____

9. Has language of instruction in reading, math, and written language been uniform in all grades?

Yes _____   No _____   Comments _____

_____

10. Peer comparison: a) How is pupil significantly different from others of similar educational, cultural, or linguistic background? b) Delays in common childhood tasks?

_____

11. Sibling comparison: How does child's progress compare to that of siblings (academically, linguistically, socially)?

_____

12. Are there any cultural or environmental factors which may affect learning?

_____

13. Describe any drastic family changes (moving, deaths) that have occurred during the child's lifetime.

_____

14. Health concerns (major health problems, medication, etc.)

_____

15. a) Degree of parent's English schooling: _____
    b) Where did parents spend childhood? _____
    c) Highest grade of school completed: father _____   mother _____

16. Did anyone in the family have learning problems? (Who?) Explain

_____

17. General comments/other relevant information (optional)

_____

Entrevista bilingüe/maestro _____

Persona entrevistada _____

APENDICE DE REFERENCIA SST
ARTICULOS CRITICOS PARA ESTUDIANTES MINORITARIOS
EN EL IDIOMA

Nombre _____ Fecha de macimiento _____

Grado _____ Fecha _____

Resultado de contactos con los padres (incluir fechas) _____

_____

_____

1. Lengua natal _____ Lengua dominante _____

2. Años en U.S. _____ País natal _____

3. Uso de lenguaje con el alumno: padres _____

   hermanos _____

   compañeros _____

   Comentarios: _____

4. Idioma dominante Exámen de Habilidad

   Exámen usado (Exámen actual) _____ Fecha _____

   Exámen usada: _____ Fecha _____

   Idioma dominante Nivel: _____

   LEP: NES _____ LES _____ FES _____

   FEP: _____

   Exámen usada: _____ Fecha _____

   Nivel: _____

   LEP: NES _____ LES _____ FES _____

   FEP: _____

5. Total de años de instrucción formal: En U.S. _____ en el país natal _____

6. Número de escuelas atendidas en U.S. _ _____

7. Asistencia: Regular _____ Irregular _____

   Comentarios: _____

8. Programa de idiomas/instrucción y servicios por nivel (circule):

Solo inglés	Pre K	K	1	2	3	4	5	6	7	8
Bilingüe	Pre K	K	1	2	3	4	5	6	7	8
BILP	Pre K	K	1	2	3	4	5	6	7	8
ELD	Pre K	K	1	2	3	4	5	6	7	8

Instructor de lectura primaria: maestro bilingual: _____   maestro diferido _____   ayudante _____

Problemas/comentarios: _____

9. Tiene instrucción en lectura, metemáticas y escritura en todos los grados.

   Si _____   No _____   Comentarios: _____

   _____

10. Comparación con los compañeros: a) Cuál es la diferencia de dicción del alumno, de otros de similar cultura?
    b) Demoras en tareas comunes de la niñez?

    _____

11. Comparación con el hermano: ¿Cómo se compara el progreso del niño al de
    los hermanos (academicamente, lenguísticamente, socialmente)?

    _____

12. ¿Hay algún factor cultural o ambiental que pueda afectar el aprendizaje?

    _____

13. Describir algún cambio drástico (mudanzas, fallecimientos) que hayan ocurrido   durante la vida del niño.

    _____

14. Preocupaciones de salud (problemas mayores de salud, medicamentos, etc.)

    _____

15. a) ¿Diploma de escuela inglesa de los padres? _____
    b) ¿Donde pasaron la niñez los padres?
    c) El grado más alto de escuela completa: padre _____   madre _____

16. Alguien de la familia ha tenido problemas de aprendizaje? (¿Quién?) Explicar

    _____

17. Comentarios generales/otra relevante información (optativo)

    _____

EQUIPO ESTUDIANTIL DE EXITO

¿Que es el Futuro?

Al término de la junta una fecha consecutiva se fijará para revisar el progreso. Una vez mas se le extenderá una cordial invitación con los miembros de la SST para evaluar los cambios y el desorrollo en el alumno.

¿Cual es el papel del Padre en el Proceso de la SST?

El Padre:

- proporciona información valiosa y ofrece otro punto de vista para planear un programa efectivo,

- comparte las fortalezas y preocupaciones del hijo/a con el personal instructivo escolar,

- participa en el desarrollo de un plan de intervención positivo para el hijo/a.

Los esfuerzas de mi niño/a son: (inter"Es, tena favorita, habilidades): _____

Preocupaciones de mi niño/a: _____

Lo que le da anima a mi niño/a es: _____

Expectatiras que you tengo/quisiera para mi niño/a son: _____

Cuestionario Estudiantil

Mis fuerzas son: _____

Cosas que me gustan de la escuela son: _____

Mis preocupaciones son: _____

En Casa

Modos en que mi familia me ayuda: _____

Mi Futuro

Cuando yo términe la escuela preparatoria, yo quisiera: _____

Trabajos que yo quisiera son: _____

Folleto del Padre

Correspondencia a este domicilio: _____

Folleto del Padre

Correspondencia a este domicilio: _____

Equipo Estudiantil dé Exito

El Distrito Escolar Unificado de Moreno Valley se compromete en proporcionar las mejores oportunidades educativas para el alumno.

Para crear el mejor medio ambiente de aprendizaje para el alumno, el Distrito Escolar Unificado de Moreno Valley ofrece un recurso educativo de una Equipo Estudiantil dé Exito (SST).

¿Que Significa Equipo Estudiantil dé Exito (SST)?

El alumno logra más éxito cuando funciona un fuerta espirtu de cooperación entre hogar y la escuela.

Basándonos sobre nuestras responsabilidades compartidas, la SST hace sus juntas en la escuela para explorar posibilidades y estrategias para mejorar y ofrecer las necesidades educativas del alumno.

¿Como Trabaja?

El Proceso:

Típicamente el alumno es referido por el maestro del salón de clase, pero cualquier personal educativo puede hacer una petición de apoyo de la SST para algún alumno cuyo aprendizaje, su comportamiento o necesidades emocionales que no estan cumplidas bajo las circunstancias existentes.

Los maestros han hecho una junta para revisar cambios en los salones de clase para intensificar el aprendizaje del alumno antes de hacer la primer junta formal con la SST. Un cambio puede ser tan sencillo como una locación nueva donde esta sentado el alumno, uno hoja de lecciones diariamente, o el aumento de uso en ayuda instructiva de ilustraciones. A veces un cambio sencillo puede ser una gran diferencia en el alumno.

Cualquier cambio que se ha intentado o que aún está al corriente, será descuido con usted en la junta de la SST. Con el uso de ésta información, la asociación puede sugerir otros procedimientos para ayudar al estudiante.

La Junta del Equipo Estudiantil de Exito:

Miembros del personal educativo van a llegar con información sobre el alumno. La información puede incluir muestras de lecciones de su trabajo, anotaciones de asistencia a la escuela o a los resultados de las colocaciones del alumno. Toda información irá registrada en la forma de resumen de la SST.

El resumen de la SST llevará el contenido en las regiones de:

- Reforzar el alumno
- Información
- Cambios
- Areas de precupación
- Preguntas
- Estrategias
- Acción
- Persona(as) de responsabilidad

Otros miembros de la asociación pueden incluir miembros del personal educativo para apoyar como la enfermera o el psicólogo y un facilitador de junta.

FORMULARIO RECORDATIVO DEL SST

ESTUDIANTE: _____ ESCUELA: _____ EQUIPO/MIEMBROS DE: _____ FECHA INICIAL DE SST: _____

IDIOMA PRINCIPAL: _____ GRADO: _____ FECHA DE NACIMIENTO: _____ PADRE DE FAMILIA: _____

INFORMACION NUEVA	ACCIONES PREVIAS	RESULTADOS	ACCIONES NUEVAS	Quién	Cuando

Fecha Recordativa: _____   Invita: _____

Firma del Miembro/Puesto:

1. Padre de familia _____   5. _____ /
2. Estudiante _____   6. _____ /
3. Administrador _____   7. _____ /
4. Maestro de Referencia _____ 8. _____ /

FORMULARIO RECORDATIVO DEL SST

ESTUDIANTE: _____ ESCUELA: _____ EQUIPO/MIEMBROS DE: _____ Fecha Inicial de SST: _____

IDIOMA PRINCIPAL: _____ GRADO: _____ FECHA DE NACIMIENTO: _____ PADRE DE FAMILIA: _____

PREOCUPACIONES PREVIAS	ACCIONES NUEVAS	Quien	Cuando

Fecha Recordativa: _____ Invita: _____

Firma del Miembro / Puesto:

1. Padre de familia _____
2. Estudiante _____
3. Administrador _____
4. Maestro de Referencia _____

5. _____ / _____
6. _____ / _____
7. _____ / _____
8. _____ / _____

School Attendence Review Team (SART)

SCHOOL ATTENTANCE REVIEW TEAM (SART)
Frequently Asked Questions

1. What is the purpose/goal of a School Attendance Review Team? (SART)

The overall goal of the SART is to improve the attendance of students at the school site. First and foremost, the SART implements positive attendance practices and incentives for students who maintain good attendance, and recognize students who improve their attendance. In order for the SART to do its job, teachers must record attendance, both daily and period by period, without fail. This is the only way to ensure accuracy of the data for the SART to utilize.

The SART is also empowered to notify parents/guardians of any unexcused absences, excessive "excused" absences, and three or more tardies of more than thirty (30) minutes on each occurrence. These notifications are typically done through the Notification of Absence letters one and two. Usually the second letter requires the parent/guardian and the student to attend a meeting with a member(s) of the SART. These meetings /conferences attempt to address the reasons for the poor attendance and develop a contract with the parent/guardian and the student. This contract will be monitored regularly. If the absences continue, the SART will send a third and fourth notification that declares the student as a "habitual truant". (Samples of these letters and contract are found following these Q and A's). When, if, the student does not improve his/her attendance, the team will decide if the matter should be referred to the School Attendance Review Board, a district/city level structure that will also work to determine the causes or the continued truancy, and to develop an agreement/contract with specific actions that must be implemented. After the school and district has made a conscientious effort to work with the student and family, and these efforts have still not been successful, the SARB will prepare the documentation to refer the matter to the local District Attorney who will put the matter on the truancy court calendar, if a truancy court calendar exists in your community. At that point, the judge has a number of options that s/he can impose at their discretion.

2. We have so many students at our school, how can we keep track of all of so many attendance histories?

All school districts have recording and tracking information devices for student attendance. Most of them will have to report that information to their respective states on a regular basis in order to obtain the funds based on the number of students attending school. Often called the "mainframe", they can print out data that will provide very valuable information to the SART. The number of days missed, excused or unexcused, tardies, class periods missed, irregular patterns that may indicate class "cutting", and history information. One high school I worked at received regular reports from the main office with the names of students by the percentage of time they were attending, and grouped by the names of their counselors. There were students attending 90-100% of the time, 80 to 90%, 70 to 80%, 60 to 70%, and those below 60%. The counselor would be the first person to do what they can to help, and then, if indicated,

---

participate with other members of the SART in a conference with parents/ guardians and the student.

It is useful if the SART creates a sort of spread sheet to track their efforts on behalf of the student. Various "interventions" are listed at the top of the spread sheet and the names of Pstudents down the side of the document. There would be a place to check off when a certain intervention has occurred. Items listed might include: phone call to parent, letters 1,2, 3,4 sent, contract signed, home visit, SST held, service referrals made, referral to SARB, etc.

3. Who should make up the members of SART?

    A team would typically be made up of a chair/facilitator who is often a member of the student support team, a counselor(s), Dropout Prevention Specialist (DPS), clerical staff at the school responsible for attendance, dean or head counselor, a school resource officer if one is serving at the school, and possibly a member of a school-based or school-linked agency that may provide services to the student. In some cities, Juvenile Probation officers are assigned to school areas so they can attend SART meeting and monitor their wards at the school site.

4. When can our SART meet?

    Much like the CARE team and the Student Success Team (SST), the SART members need to be very flexible to find times to meet. Most of the SART personnel do not have classroom responsibilities, and hopefully they can work out a time that is convenient for the majority of them. When a particular parent/guardian is coming in for a conference, all other members of the SART should be informed so they can decide if they should attend.

BERKELEY UNIFIED SCHOOL DISTIRCT
FIRST NOTIFICTION OF TRUANCY OR EXCESSIVE ABSENCES

Date: _____ School: _____

Dear Parent/Guardian:

This letter is to inform you that your child/student_____ in the
_____ grade, is considered a truant.

Unjustified Absences:

California Education Section 48260 – Any student subject to full-time education who is absent from school without a valid excuse for more than three days or tardy in excess of 30 minutes on each of more than three occasions in one school year is a truant.

California Education Section 48260.5

(A). Upon a pupil's initial classification as a truant, the school district shall notify the students' parent/guardian by first class mail or other reasonable means, of the following:

(1) That the pupil/student is truant.

(2) That the parent/guardian is obligated to compel the attendance of the pupil at school.

(3) That the parents/guardians who fail to meet this obligation may be guilty of an infraction and subject to prosecution pursuant to Article 6 (commencing with Section 48290) of Chapter 2 of Part 27.

(B). The district also should inform the parent/guardians of the following:

(1) Alternative educational programs available in the district.

(2) The right to meet with appropriate school personnel to discuss solutions to the students' truancy.

(3) The student may e subject to arrest under Education Code Section 48264.

(4) The student may be subject to suspension, restriction, or delay of his/her driving privlidge, pursuant to Vehicle Code 13202.7

(5) That it is recommended that the parent or guardian accompany the student to school and attend classes with the student for one day. (Added Statutes, 1983, Chapter 498).

Excessive Excused Absences: (Please attach attendance record to this notification)

Truant, unverified, unexcused , excessive excused absences, and tardies affect the student's education and increase the chances of school failure. Tardies interrupt the classroom and in interfere with the learning environment for all students. Please discuss this issue with your child. Failure to improve his/her attendance will result in a conference with the School Attendance Review Team at the school.

Our goal is to educate your child. We cannot be successful if your child is not in school.

Administrator's Signature:_____School: _____Date:_____

Attached copy of attendance record, cc: cumulative file, School Attendance Review Board, Student Services

BERKELEY UNIFIED SCHOOL DISTRICT
SECOND NOTIFICATION OF TRUANCY OR EXCESSIVE ABSENSES

Student's name:_____ ____Grade:_____School:_____

Parent(s)/Guardian(s) name:_____

Address:_____ Zip code: _____Student ID#._____

Dear Parent(s)/Guardian(s):

This **SECOND LETTER** is to inform you that your child/student continues to have an attendance problem.

Number of excused absences:_____

Number of unexcused absences:_____

Number of tardies (31+ minutes: _____

Total: _____ (Please attach a copy of the attendance record)

1. The School Attendance Review Team (SART) has received a referral on behalf of your child/student regarding excessive excused absences, tardies, or unexcused absenses.
2. An appointment has been made for you and your child/student to meet with the SART to consider a proper plan for improvement.
3. Both parents are expected to attend if at all possible. Please bring your child/student.

YOUR SCHEDULED APPOINTMENT IS AS FOLLOWS:

Date: _____
Time: _____
Location: _____

If for any reason that this time and date is not possible for you please contact:

_____

Failure to appear will result in a referral for further action. Please be prompt for the appointment
California Education Code Section 48261 – "Subsequent Report of Truancy. Any pupil/student who has been reported as a truant and who is again absent from school without a valid excuse one or more days or tardy on one or more days, shall again be reported as a truant to the attendance supervisor or to the superintendent of the district."

Principal or designee: _____Date: _____
Attached Copy of Attendance Record, cc: Cumulative folder/student's teachers, SART, Student Services

BERKELEY UNIFIED SCHOOL DISTRICT
THIRD NOTIFICATION OF TRUANCY
School:_____

Date: _____Regarding: _____Grade:_____

Dear Parent/Guardian/Caregiver:

Your child/student has received a First Notification of Truancy or Excessive Absences and a Second Notification of Truancy or Excessive Absences for the current school semester. This third letter informs you that your child is considered a habitual truant.

The additional number and dates of truancies since the second letter are:

Number of unexcused absences:_____Dates: _____

Number of tardies (31+minutes) _____ Dates: _____

History of Attendance for the current semester:

Attached attendance record as of enrollment date of: _____is as follows:

Days of enrollment:_____Days present: _____Tardies (31+ minutes)_____

Days of unexcused absences:_____Days of excused absences: _____

California Education Code Section 48262 – Habitual Truant: Any pupil/student deemed a habitual truant and has been reported as a truant three or more ties per school year, provided that no pupil/student shall be deemed a habitual truant unless an appropriate district officer or employee has made a conscientious effort to hold at least one conference with a parent or guardian of the pupil/student and the pupil/student himself or herself after filing of either of the reports required of California Education Code Section 48260 or 48261.

The school has attempted to work with you and to solve your child's attendance problems. Unfortunately these attempts have not been successful. It will now be necessary for you t o attend a hearing with the School Attendance Review Board, made up of both District and community based staff. You will be receiving a separate letter as to the time and location of the this hearing. Failure to attend this meeting may result in further action.

A parent/guardian who fails to meet his/her obligations may be found guilty of an infraction and subject to prosecution (California Education Code Section 48290). Complaints filed with filed with the District Attorney may go to court and result in fines or other court ordered consequences.

Signature of Principal or designee: _____date: _____
Cc: Cumulative file, School Attendance Review Team, Office of Student Services

BERKELEY UNIFIED SCHOOL DISTRICT
FORTH NOTIFICATION OF TRUANCY (HABITUAL TRUANT)

Date:_____Student:_____Grade:_____

Dear Parent/Guardian/Caregiver:

Your child/student was last reported as truant on: _____This is the fourth letter informing you that your child/student is considered a habitual truant.

Additional date(s) of truancies (at least one additional)

Unexcused: _____Tardies: (31+minutes)_____

History of attendance:
Attendance record as of: _____ **is as follows:**

Days of enrollment: _____   Days present: _____

Unexcused absences:_____Excused absences: _____Taries: _____

California Education Code Section 48262 – Habitual Truant: Any pupil/student deemed a habitual truant and who has been reported as a truant three or more time per school year, provided that no pupil/ student shall be deemed a habitual truant unless an appropriate district officer or employee has made a conscientious effort to hold at least one conference with the parent or guardian of the pupil/student and the student himself or herself after filing of either of the reports required under California Education Code Section 48260 or 48261.

Unfortunately, our efforts to work with you and your son/daughter to address their attendance issues have not been successful thus far. Please know that, like you, we have the best interests of your child/student as our primary goal. We know that excessive absence in school can not only lead to academic failure, but the research is clear that poor attendance often leads to dropping out of school altogether. In this competitive labor market, we know that a high school diploma is considered by most as a minimum requirement.

We are in the process of collecting the necessary documentation to refer this matter to the District Attorney so that it can be placed on the court calendar to be heard before a judge. The judge has the discretion to impose various consequences as they deem appropriate.

If, before us sending this matter to the District Attorney, you would like to meet with the School Attendance Review Board, please contact: _____at: _____

If we do not hear from you within ten days, this matter will be referred on to legal authorities.

Signature of Principal:_____School_____Date:_____
Cc: Cumulative file, School Attendance Review Team, Office of Student Services

Berkeley Unified School District
Attendance Contract for Student and Family
School Attendance Review Team (SART)

Student_____School_____date_____

At this time, having met in conference with the parent(s)/guardian(s) of the student, the School Attendance Review Team believes that the student would benefit from the recommended actions listed below instead of being referred to the Student Attendance Review Board (SARB), and possible court action.

Therefore, the following parent/guardian, student and school actions are agreed upon:

1. Attend school each day and come prepared to participate.
2. Remain in school for the full day, and attend every period, as appropriate.
3. Present to the school a note from a doctor/nurse to verify any past or future absences due to illness.
4. Follow all school rules and regulations and maintain appropriate behavior.
5. Parent/guardian is aware of their legal obligation for their child to regularly attend school.
6. _____
7. _____
8. _____
9. _____
10. _____

Parent(s)/Guardian(s): I/We consent to the participation of my/our child under the agreement above, and I/we will cooperate and support this attendance improvement plan, as outlined. I/we further consent to the exchange of information and relevant student records between the school and the agencies/services to which my/our child is referred.

Please note who is responsible for each action item, and when this will occur, if indicated.

Parent(s)/Guardian(s) signature: _____date_____

Student: I have received a copy of this agreement and understand the terms and agree to comply with all of conditions above: _____date_____

School administrator signature: _____ date_____

Progress report due on: _____

cc: Parent/Guardian, Student,cumulative folder, and Student Services Department

Components of Successful Alternative Programs

COMPONENTS OF SUCCESSFUL ALTERNATIVE PROGRAMS

1. **Individualized Instruction**
    The curriculum is tailored to the needs of the students. Teaching, tutoring, and counseling activities are geared toward the individual needs of the students.

2. **Reward System**
    Many alternative programs attach certain rewards with effort and achievement. For instance a student with a truancy problem may be rewarded for attending 10 full days in a row. Rewards could be food coupons, leisure time or other activities of interest to students.

3. **Clear Discipline Policy**
    Alternative programs establish a "bottom line" for acceptable behavior and involvement.

4. **Freedom to Learn at One's Own Speed**
    Many alternative programs avoid grade level designation and instead offer contract learning in which tasks are clear and can be completed quickly.

5. **Use of High Interest Materials**
    These materials vary from vocational information to survival skills.

6. **Variations in Seat Time and Scheduling**
    Allowing students to attend at night and the weekends in addition to pursuing studies outside the classroom are viable options in alternative programs.

7. **Work Experience and Exposure**
    Offering students internships, paid and non-paid work and exposure to the work world are important components of alternative programs.

8. **Variations in Locations**
    The physical space in which a student learns may vary. Students are allowed to study in different settings to stimulate discussion and inquiry.

9. **Human Scale**
    Most alternative programs are characterized by small groupings and intimate settings.

10. **Caring Staff**
    Forty-eight percent of the drop out sample in the research conducted by the Citizens Policy Center cited "better teachers" or "more teachers who cared" as the changes they would like to see in the schools.

11. **Student Involvement**
    Many drop out students have been out of school in the adult world. They need to be treated as adults. Activities to increase their attachment to the school is critical. Student involvement provides an environment for students to be treated as adults and to develop a commitment to the school.

12. **Counselling Components**
    As a result of budget cuts counselors have been eliminated in many high schools. Alternative programs rely heavily on a counselor - student relationship.

References

Chapter 1

1. Balfanz, R., and Byrnes, V., Chronic Absenteeism: Summarizing What We Know From Nationally Available Data, Baltimore, Johns Hopkins University Center for Social Organization, 2012, pages 1–29.
2. Rumberger, Russell, Dropping Out: Why Students Drop Out of High School and What Can Be Done About It, Cambridge, Massachusetts, and London, England, Harvard University Press, 2011, pages 169–206.
3. Smink, Jay, and Schargel, Franklin P., Helping Students Graduate: A Strategic Approach to Dropout Prevention, Larchmont, New York, Eye on Education, 2004, page 9.

Chapter 3

1. The Dalai Lama, and Howard C. Cutler, The Art of Happiness: A Handbook for Living, London, England, Hodder and Stoughton (An Hachette UK company), 2009, page 69.

Chapter 5

1. National PTA, Where Have All the Students Gone, Chicago, Illinois, From Our Children Magazine, 1979.
2. DeWitt, Peter, and Slade, Sean, School Climate Change: How to Build a Positive Environment for Learning, Alexandria, Virginia, Association for Curriculum and Supervision Development, 2014.
3. Adapted from Ramsey, R. D., Educator's Discipline Handbook, Negative School Climate Indicators, Upper Saddle River, New Jersey, Prentice Hall, Inc., 1981.
4. Thacker, Tony, Bell, John S., and Schargel, Franklin P., Creating School Cultures That Embrace Learning: What Successful Leaders Do, Larchmont, New York, Eye on Education, 2009, pages 19–21.
5. Thacker, Tony, Bell, John S., and Schargel, Franklin P., Creating School Cultures That Embrace Learning: What Successful Leaders Do, Larchmont, New York, Eye on Education, 2009, page 19.
6. Freiburg, H. J., unknown origin.
7. Gonzales, Luis D., School Climate: 180 Degree Turn, Negative to Positive, Los Angeles, California, Division of Evaluation, Attendance and Pupil Services, Los Angeles County Office of Education (date unknown).
8. Werner, Emmy E., and Smith, Ruth S., Vulnerable But Invincible: A Study of Resilient Children and Youth, Chicago, Illinois, McGraw Hill, 1982 (reprinted in 2013).
9. Edmonds, Ron, The School Achievement of Minority Children, Mahwah, New Jersey, Lawrence Erlbaum Associates, Inc., 1986.

10. Thacker, Tony, Bell, John, and Schargel, Franklin P., Creating School Cultures That Embrace Learning: What Successful Leaders Do, Larchmont, New York, Eye on Education, 2009, page 69.
11. Preble, Bill, Solutions to the Dropout Crisis, a webinar series by the National Dropout Prevention Network/Center, entitled School Climate Through Students' Eyes: How School Climate Affects Student Learning, April 3, 2010.
12. Jennings, K., former Deputy Assistant Secretary and Director of Safe and Drug Free Schools, U.S. Department of Education, quoted statement. National conference on Bullying in Orlando, Florida on 02/14/2011.
13. Wehlage, Gary G., and Rutter, Robert A., Dropping Out: How Much Do Schools Contribute to the Problem?, Madison, Wisconsin, Wisconsin Center for Educational Research, 1985.
14. Weis, Lois, Farrar, Eleanor, and Petrie, Hugh G., Dropouts from School: Issues, Dilemmas, and Solutions, State University of New York Press, State University Plaza, Albany, New York, ISBN-0-7914—0109-x, 1989, Chapter 1 by Gary G. Wehlage, pages 1–11.
15. Ginot, Haim G., Between Parent and Child, New York, New York, Three Rivers Press, 1965 (revised and updated in 2003 by Dr. Alice Ginott and Dr. Wallace Goddard).
16. Baumeister, Donald, Social Work Department, spoken quote, California State University, Los Angeles, 2009.
17. Blonsky, Howard, The Teachers Role in Fostering Resiliency and Mental Health in Children, and Help in Overcoming Emotional Difficulties, unpublished paper, 2016.

Chapter 6

1. Dupper, David R., A New Model of School Discipline: Engaging Students and Preventing Behavior Problems, New York, New York, Oxford University Press, School Social Work Association of America, Oxford Workshop Series, Preface, 2010.
2. Anyon, Yolanda, Attebrry-Ash, Brittanie, Yang, Jessica, Pauline, Malina, Pauline, Wiley, Katherine, Cash, Donna, Downing, Barbara, Greer, Eldridge, and Pisciotta, Lisa, It's All About Relationships: Educators' Rationales and Strategies for Building Connections with Students to Prevent Exclusionary School Discipline Outcomes, Washington, D.C., National Association of Social Workers Press, Children and Schools Journal, Vol. 40, Issue 4, October 2018, pages 221–230.
3. Orlando, Marco, Berta, Steve, Blonsky, Howard, Butler, Vicki, Deeb, Bill, and Stetkevich, Andy, Student Success Teams: Parents, School, Community, Soquel, California, EduAlliance Network, 2000, page 76.

Chapter 7

1. Gonzales, Luis D., The Prevention of Truancy: Programs and Strategies That Address the Problems of Truancy and Dropouts, Los Angeles, California, Division of Evaluation, Attendance and Pupil Services, Los Angeles County Office of Education (date unknown).
2. Barr, Robert D., and Parrett, William, Poor and Minority Students Achieve High Academic Performance, notes from a keynote address at the 15th annual Dropout Prevention Conference, 2005.

3. Schargel, Franklin P., and Smink, Jay, Strategies to Help Solve Our School Dropout Problem, Larchmont, New York, Eye on Education, 2001, pages 39–44.

4. Inventory of Policies and Practices Related to Student Failure and Dropping Out, Iowa Department of Education, 1989.

5. Rumberger, Russell, Dropping Out: Why Students Drop Out of High School and What Can be Done About It?, Cambridge, Massachusetts, and London, England, Harvard University Press, 2011, pages 32–36.

Chapter 8

1. Curran Neild R., Falling Off Track During the Transition to High School, Published by the David and Lucile Packard Foundation, The Future of Children, Vol. 19, No. 1, Spring 2009. Princeton University, Princeton, New Jersey.

2. Quint, Janet, Thompson, Saskia Levy, Bald, Margaret, Relationships, Rigor and Readiness: Strategies for Improving High Schools, The Council of Great City Schools and the National High School Alliance, New York, NY, 2008.

3. Saunders, Marisa, Silber, David, and Zarate, Estela, What Factors Predict High School Graduation Rates in the Los Angeles Unified School District?, California Dropout Research Project, UC Santa Barbara, Gevirtz Graduate School of Education, Santa Barbara, CA, 2008.

4. Chief Sealth High School, Seattle, Washington, Description of their 9th-grade comprehensive orientation program, 1989.

5. Balfanz, Robert, Can the American High School Become an Avenue of Advancement for All?, Published by the David and Lucille Packard Foundation, The Future of Children, Vol. 19, Issue 1, Spring 2009, page 22.

6. Foreman, Tabitha, Ninth Grade Walk Through, Virginia Department of Education (date unknown).

Chapter 9

1. Taylor, Linda, and Adelman, Howard, UCLA School Mental Health Program, Bi-Weekly Newsletter Focusing on the Re-engagement of Out of School Youth, October 2018 edition.

2. Martin, Nancy, and Halperin, Samuel, Whatever It Takes: How Twelve Communities are Reconnecting Out-of- School Youth, Chapter 1, Montgomery County (Dayton, Ohio), Out of School Youth Task Force, Deborah Feldman, chair, Montgomery County Administrator, feldmand@mcohio.org, and Michael Carter, Director Sinclair Fast Forward Center, Michael.carter@sinclair.edu, American Youth Policy Forum, 2006.

Chapter 10

1. Cash, Terry, and Duttweiler, Patricia, Cloud, Planning, Collaboration, and Implementation Strategies for Truancy Programs, Truancy Prevention in Action Series, National Dropout Prevention Center/Network, 2005.

2. Student Success Through Collaboration: A Policy Statement of the Council of Chief State School Officers, Washington, DC, 1992.

3. Karasoff, Patricia, Blonsky, Howard, Perry, Kris, and Schear, Tracy, Integrated and Collaborative Services: A Technical Assistance Planning Guide, California Research Institute, San Francisco State University, 1996, an unpublished manual.

Chapter 12

1. Every Student, Every Day, A toolkit developed by the Federal Department of Education to support the Every Student Succeeds Act, 2015. Download document at: http://www2.ed.gov/about/inits/ed/chronicabsenteeism/toolkit.pdf.
2. Smink, Jay, and Schargel, Franklin P., Helping Students Graduate: A Strategic Approach to Dropout Prevention, Larchmont, New York, Eye on Education, 2004.
3. Schargel, Franklin P., and Smink, Jay, Strategies to Help Solve Our School Dropout Problem, Larchmont, New York, Eye on Education, 2001, pages 40–44.
4. Rumberger, Russell, Dropping Out: Why Students Drop Out of High School and What Can Be Done About It?, Cambridge, Massachusetts, and London, England, Harvard University Press, 2011, pages 210–229.
5. Graduating Great Kids: Baltimore Public Schools, Extracted from the Comprehensive Plan to Address the High Number of Students Dropping Out, Baltimore, Maryland, 2010.
6. Dropout Prevention/School Completion Invention Resource Guide, Maryland State Department of Education, 2011.

Index

Tables and boxes are indicated by *t* and *b* following the page number

For the benefit of digital users, indexed terms that span two pages (e.g., 52–53) may, on occasion, appear on only one of those pages.